本书受四川农业大学"双支计划"资助

经济管理学术文库·经济类

小农户参与可持续土地利用决策比较研究

A Comparative Study of Small Farmers'
Participation in Decision-making on
Sustainable Land Use

何　格　[埃塞] 阿布勒姆·特泽拉·格塞斯／著

经济管理出版社
ECONOMY & MANAGEMENT PUBLISHING HOUSE

图书在版编目（CIP）数据

小农户参与可持续土地利用决策比较研究/何格，［埃塞］阿布勒姆·特泽拉·格塞斯
著.—北京：经济管理出版社，2019.8
ISBN 978 - 7 - 5096 - 6758 - 3

Ⅰ.①小…　Ⅱ.①何…②阿…　Ⅲ.①农户—土地利用—对比研究—中国、埃塞俄比亚
Ⅳ.①F301.24 ②F342.111

中国版本图书馆 CIP 数据核字（2019）第 149124 号

组稿编辑：郭　飞
责任编辑：张巧梅
责任印制：黄章平
责任校对：张晓燕

出版发行：经济管理出版社
　　　　　（北京市海淀区北蜂窝 8 号中雅大厦 A 座 11 层　100038）
网　　　址：www. E - mp. com. cn
电　　　话：（010）51915602
印　　　刷：北京晨旭印刷厂
经　　　销：新华书店
开　　　本：720mm×1000mm/16
印　　　张：12.25
字　　　数：210 千字
版　　　次：2019 年 9 月第 1 版　　2019 年 9 月第 1 次印刷
书　　　号：ISBN 978 - 7 - 5096 - 6758 - 3
定　　　价：68.00 元

前　言

　　土地是财富之母，是人类社会经济发展不可或缺的重要生产、生活、生态资源。作为一种有限的、不可再生的耗竭性生计资源，土地也是财富代际转移的金融保障。土地是人们生活水平、财富多寡以及社会地位的象征，因此人地关系问题是人类社会发展进程中普遍被关注的话题。在由农业经济向工业经济转型的发展中，国家获得并保有足够的农业用地仍然是保障粮食安全、维系经济增长和促进社会进步取得成功的重要途径。因此，土地利用及管理方式对一个国家尤其是发展中国家的未来具有重大影响。随着全球人口的急剧增加，人均农业土地占有量迅速下降，农业土地的细碎化成为发展中国家农业经营中普遍面临的问题。土地细碎化不仅造成农户经营规模的减小以及规模不经济，而且带来预期不稳定以及产权不安全。而土地的细碎化和产权的不安全又影响土地使用者的长期性投资，这对扩大农业规模化生产和农业生产效率的提升都有重大影响。自从第二次世界大战以来，通过土地整理减小农业用地的细碎化程度，从而为规模化经营和农业生产效率的提升提供前提和保障已成为世界各国普遍采用的实现土地资源可持续利用管理的重要手段。

　　中国和埃塞俄比亚同为发展中国家，两国在农业生产经营制度的安排以及土地制度的安排上有相似之处。在改革开放前，两国农业经济发展均处于贫困状态，均以小规模自给农业为主。根据两国宪法和土地管理法，土地资源由政府管理控制，农民、土地所有者及农村集体经济组织拥有长期的土地使用权。随着中国 20 世纪 70 年代末和埃塞俄比亚 20 世纪 90 年代初经济改革的推进，农业经济在 GDP 中的相对份额开始逐年增长。在过去几十年中，以每年 10% 的增长率快速增长，并使大量依靠土地获得生活来源的农村贫困人口摆脱贫困。然而，在两国的许多农村地区，特别是在埃塞俄比亚，土地细碎化带来的粮食不安全仍然是未来经济社会发展面临的重大挑战。中国之所以能以地球 7% 的耕地养活了 22% 的世界人口，主要经验是改革开放以来通过小农户参与土地整理，实现优化土地利用制度、维护农业用地、最大限度地提高农业生产多重社会经济目标，进而实现小农户的可持续生计和农村经济社会的可持续发展。这为埃塞俄比亚推进土地整理提供了宝贵的经验借鉴。

为比较研究中国和埃塞俄比亚小农户参与农业土地整理以及对土地细碎化的意识、感知和适应意愿，从而为两个研究区域的土地资源可持续利用和管理提供有用的决策信息，本书选取中国四川省和埃塞俄比亚中部高地为研究对象，首先研究了农业用地细碎化如何影响农业生产效率，再进一步研究哪些因素影响小农户参与土地整理，从而实现土地资源可持续利用管理的意识、感知和适应意愿。运用随机前沿分析（SFA）和数据包络分析（DEA）等定量分析方法对四川省和埃塞俄比亚中部高原地区小农户的粮食生产效率的定量研究结果表明：耕地规模、劳动力和资本均为正，对四川省粮食产量有显著预测作用。此外，四川省小农户的粮食生产技术效率为 73%，而埃塞俄比亚中部高地的小农户则有 50% 的技术、60% 的配置和 30% 的经济效率。与埃塞俄比亚中部高地相比，四川省小农户的技术效率更高，但在这两个研究领域，仍有更多的空间来进一步提高效率。耕地规模、灌溉、良种、肥料、农药均为正，显著提高了四川小农户的技术效率。在埃塞俄比亚中部高地，土地破碎化、作物多样性和地块数量对小农户的技术效率具有负向预测作用，而梯田、耕作、病虫害管理和土地休耕显著提高了小农户的技术效率。

运用结构方程模型（SEM）等定量研究方法对影响小农户参与土地整理，从而实现土地资源可持续利用管理的意识、感知和适应意愿的研究结果发现：电子和印刷媒介对四川的小农户参与土地整理，从而实现土地资源可持续利用管理的意识、感知和适应意愿的影响是微不足道的。因此，当地政府部门更会使用媒体特别是当地报纸和互联网授权，促进土地整理项目的努力在四川省的农村地区以及提高当地农民的意识、感知和适应，目的是提高农业生产效率，实现农村可持续发展。而除洪水、干旱、气候变化、土地退化和土壤侵蚀问题外，土地破碎化是埃塞俄比亚农业经济的主要威胁之一。了解当地农民对土地破碎化的看法和适应意愿，对于政策制定者规划和实施土地整理等综合土地管理工具至关重要。然而，埃塞俄比亚还没有开始全面的土地整理。因此，现在正是国家决策者为提高农业生产效率、实现农村可持续发展而规划和实施土地综合整治的正确时机。

Table of Contents

I. General Introduction

1.1 Background

Land is a finite non – reproducible consumable resource of livelihood and a financial security transferred as wealth across generations (Ellis, 1992) . The relationship between the land and the people is profound as people's living standard, wealth, social status and aspirations. In developing agrarian society access to agricultural land remains as a vital resource to success for food – security as well as economic growth and development. Thus, the way the land governed and administered therefore has a significant impact on a country's future.

The agricultural economy and development of China and Ethiopia were poor and highly dominated by small – scaled subsistence rural farming system before the opening – up of the economic reform. However, with the onset of the economic reform in the late 1970's in China and early 1990's in Ethiopia, the relative share of the agricultural economy in the country's gross domestic product (GDP) began increasing annually. Hence, spectacular fast economic growth has been increased with approximate 10 percent annual GDP increment in the past decades and escape hundreds of thousands of people from poverty (Gessesse et al., 2017; Solomon and Mansberger, 2003). However, land tenure and food insecurity at household level still the challenges and remain as issues in many rural areas of both countries particularly in Ethiopia.

According to the China and Ethiopia constitutions and land management laws, the land resource is controlled by the state government and the farmers/landholders have only the use right. In China the land in the urban region is owned by the central government (state) while in rural regions it is owned by the collective economic organization according to the laws and regulations otherwise they belong to the state (Li Ling and David Isaac, 1994; Benjamin and Brandt, 2002; He Ge, 2012). Thus, cities, towns, large forest areas and some farmlands are owned under state whereas, lands in rural areas and small towns which are not governed by state are owned by the rural collective organization. While in the Ethiopian situation, the right to ownership of rural and urban lands as well as of all natural resources is exclusively vested in the State and the peoples of Ethiopia. Which means that, land is a common property of the nations, nationalities and peoples of Ethiopia and shall not be subject to sale or other means of exchanges (FDRE, 1995). Hence, Chinese landholders obtain a contract land use rights for a definite period whereas, Ethiopian landholders acquire the land use right for an indefinite period in the scope of laws and they cannot sell and transfer (lease and mortgage) their land use rights to others.

In recent decades, the per – capita landholding size is decreasing rapidly across the globe (FAO, 2001) and the situation more explained in China and Ethiopia (Zhong and Ping, 2014; EEA, 2002). The landholding size gradually decreasing when they are splits into small parcel and irregular shape. The process becomes more difficult when a fragmented landholding is further fragmented into several small parcels at the same time and cause land tenure insecurity. Thus, due to land tenure insecurity and fragmentation the rural landholder farmers in China and Ethiopia are skeptical to invest long – term investment in land management practices (such as tree planting, construction of anti – erosion barriers, building of ditches and furrows) and obstacle for modern agricultural mechanization (Li, 1995; Nguyen et al., 1996; Wu et al., 2005; Tan et al., 2006; EEA, 2002) which has major threat to the agricultural production as well as efficiency.

Since the end of World War Ⅱ, land consolidation become a worldwide phenomenon and many developed and developing countries are planning and implementing a comprehensive land consolidation program as an innovative land management tool to overcome the impact of land fragmentation problems and to achieve significant results in agricultural production as well as sustainable rural development (Thomas, 2006). Land consolidation is a kind of land reform, but the objectives are different. Land reform is the redistribution of land in national or regional level to achieve social equity in terms of land ownership and use right, while land consolidation is the redistribution of land in a particular locality aiming to achieve an optimal land tenure structure to facilitate rural agricultural development (King and Burton, 1983; Thomas, 2006). According to FAO (2003) and Vitikainen (2004) land consolidation primarily focused on the creation of competitive agricultural production by enabling farmers to have larger and better shaped farm fields rather that of fragmented and small farm parcels; protection of the environment, landscape and nature; and creation of clean and tidy villages to improve the living and working conditions of rural area residents apparently to achieve sustainable rural development. In China, the traditional land consolidation was implemented during the eleventh century (Wang, 1997) and in the fourteenth century in Europe (Van Dijk, 2003). The modern land consolidation was introduced in the late nineteenth and early twentieth century. In China, the modern land consolidation was begun in the late 1990's after the establishment of Land Consolidation and Rehabilitation Center (LCRC) to maintain agricultural farmlands and ensure food security. Since then hundred thousand of rural poor quality farmland areas reclaimed every year (Zhong and Ping, 2014). However, there is no evidence yet on land consolidation in Ethiopia, while the government permits in voluntary basis. Therefore, this PhD research work attempted to evaluate the perspectives and adaptation intention of land fragmentation and consolidation well as the production efficiency of smallholder farmers in Sichuan province and in the Central Highlands of Ethiopia. Thus, this research work hopeful might contribute to Ethiopian agricultural development policy by innovating land management tool to achieve food security at the country as well as at the household level.

1. 2　Statement of the problem

The conversion of agricultural land to urban and industrial development is one of the critical processes of change in the developing economies undergoing urbanization, industrialization and globalization (He et al., 2012). In the past decades significant areas of agricultural lands are converted to urban and industrial constructions to meet the demand of economic growth and development in China and Ethiopia. That is why in recent years the contribution of the agricultural sector to the country's economic growth and development is decreasing in both countries (Wang et al., 2014; Gessesse et al. , 2017) .

Deeply rooted in the concept of sustainable development today, the efficient utilization of agricultural land is an important foundation to realize the sustainable social economy. However, at the present time the global agricultural land becomes a scare resource due to rapid population growth, industrial and urban developments, environmental and bio – physical aspects as well as institutional related issues, particularly in China and Ethiopia (Tan et al. , 2006; Wu et al. , 2005; EEA, 2002) . The situation is further explained by the partition of the agricultural lands to smaller and smaller parcels which are obstacles for modern agricultural mechanization, irrigation and drainage systems, production efficiency as well as sustainable rural development.

Land fragmentation is obvious in many areas of the world and the smallest and fragmented landholding is found in mainly in Asian and African countries. China and Ethiopia are among the top smallest and fragmented agricultural landholding countries in the world. The existence of fragmented landholdings in China and Ethiopia has a long history. The main reasons for small and fragmented agricultural landholdings in these countries are the distribution of agricultural land in terms of land quality, distance, agroecology and family size (Lin, 1992; Tan et al. , 2006; Nega et al. , 2003) . Recent studies indicated that the average number of parcels per household in China is six parcels, whereas twelve parcels in Ethiopia (Tan et al. , 2006; ERSS, 2013) .

Many empirical studies have been carried out on the potential impact of land fragmentation in agricultural productions by scholars and researchers. The outcome of these research works is categorized into two groups. The first group of scholars found that land fragmentation has a negative impact on agricultural production as well as household income (Nguyen et al. , 1996; Tan et al. , 2008; Studies, 2003; Niroula and Thapa, 2005; Thomas, 2006; Hung et al. , 2007; Rahman and Rahman, 2009; Bizimana et al. , 2004) . Whereas, the second group of researchers noted that land fragmentation has a potential benefit in risk minimization and crop diversity (King and Burton, 1982; Blarel et al. , 1992) . However, there is a research gap in the farmers' attitude, perceptions and adaptive intentions towards land fragmentation, particularly in the study areas. Thus, this PhD research work ascertain to understand the farmers land fragmentation adaptive intention in addition to production efficiency. It seems this sentence don't confront to the topic of this dissertation. You must explain the relationship between land sustainable use and land consolidation.

Since 1998 China has invested a large amount of manpower, material and financial resources in land consolidation programs and achieved a remarkable result in reclaiming poor quality soils into medium and high quality, merging small and fragmented parcels change to larger and better shape, installing agricultural infrastructures such as irrigation and drainage systems, road network to improve the agricultural production and achieve sustainable rural development in many project areas, especially in the Sichuan province. However, there is still has a number of heavy quantities, light quality, divorced from reality the pursuit of high quality design error prone to ecological damage (Wang et al. , 2014) . In addition, studies on the performance evaluation of land consolidation in the smallholder farmers' production efficiency are limited. Further, there is information gaps on the farmers' perspectives and adaptive intention on land consolidation and rehabilitation program in the study areas. Therefore, this PhD research work is carried out to investigate the impact of land consolidation on the smallholder farmers' production efficiency so well as to explore the local farmers awareness, perception and adaptation intentions towards land consolidation. I suggest you intregrate the two paragragh into one to make the reason of you choose this topic more reasonable.

1. 3　Significance of the study

China feeds 22 percent of the world population with only seven percent of the Earth's arable land. However, a large size agricultural land is utilized for urban and industrial constructions. Thus, greatest emphasis has necessary for optimal land use system to maintain the agricultural lands and maximize agricultural production as well as achieve rural livelihood and sustainable development. In this regard, a participatory comprehensive land consolidation plays a significant role on optimization of land tenure structure and urban – rural development; creating a competitive agricultural production and clean and tidy villages, and maintaining of agricultural lands. The present PhD thesis is designed to understand the preference and adaptive intentions of Sichuan smallholder farmers towards land consolidation and rehabilitation programs that implementing in their village and examine their production efficiency. Pls explain that Sichuan province account for an important role in chines agricultural sector to response to the topic of "Sichuan provience" .

Whereas, the Ethiopian agriculture is the foundation of the country's economy of which account half percent of the annual GDP, earn more than 80 percent of exports, and employ 80 percent of the total employment. However, the sector is still stagnant and subsistence due to social, economic, institutional and environmental factors. Thus, this PhD thesis is intended to comprehend the perspective and adaptation intentions of land fragmentation and its impact on production efficiency on smallholder farmers of the Central Highlands Ethiopia.

In general, this PhD research work is designed to generate information on sustainable utilization and management of land resource for both study areas by understanding the local farmers' awareness, perception and adaptation intentions towards land consolidation and fragmentation in China and Ethiopia, particularly for Sichuan and the Central Highlands of Ethiopia, respectively.

1.4　Research objectives

1.4.1　General objective

The overall purpose of this PhD research work is to understand the perspectives and adaptation intentions as well as examine the production efficiency of local farmers' under land consolidation and fragmentation scenarios in Sichuan province and in Central Highlands of Ethiopian.

1.4.2　Specific objectives

The specific objectives of this PhD thesis are:

(1) To understand the awareness, perception and adaptation intention of Sichuan smallholder farmers on land consolidation and rehabilitation;

(2) To explore the local farmers perspective and adaptation intention behavior towards land fragmentation in the Central Highlands of Ethiopia;

(3) To assess, examine and compare the smallholder farmers production efficiency and its determinants in Sichuan province and the Central Highlands of Ethiopia;

(4) To test the applicability of Structural Equation Modeling (SEM) as a tool to understand the adaptation intention of smallholder farmers towards sustainable land resource management.

1.5   Research hypothesis

The present PhD thesis formalized expectations on the production efficiency and adaptation intentions of smallholder farmers towards land fragmentation and consolidation into the following main hypotheses.

(1) Smallholder farmers perceived and aware of land fragmentation risks are more anticipated for adaptation intentions;

(2) Smallholder farmers perceived and aware of land consolidation and rehabilitation program are more intended to use modern agricultural technologies;

(3) Land fragmentation has a negative impact on the smallholder farmers production efficiency.

1.6   Conceptual framework

To achieve the objectives and test the hypothesis of this PhD thesis work a Structural Equation Modeling (SEM) technique was broadly utilized. The SEM helps the researchers to measure the direct, indirect and the total effect of the constructed inde-

pendent variables to the dependent variables. In addition, it helps to examine the association between the exogenous observed/measured variables and the indigenous latent/
unobserved variables. Thus, the conceptual framework of this study sub – divided into
three.

The first framework of this study is that, the relationship between media, social
network, awareness and perception of land consolidation to adaptation intentions. Thus,
the research synthesized to assess the contribution of media and social networks in the
development of smallholder farmers awareness and perception towards land consolidation
as well as their adaptation intentions. In addition, to what extent the perception and
awareness of land consolidation affects the adaptation intention of the Sichuan province
smallholder farmers.

The second stance of the study framework is the association of land fragmentation
risk perception, subjective norm, adaptation behavior/measure, and social incentives
to the intention/motivation of smallholder farmers towards land fragmentation. In addition, the exogenous observed/measured variables such as farmland size, number of
plots, Simpson's index and Shannon crop diversity index impact on smallholder farmers
mitigation decision also evaluated.

Once the adaptation intention of the smallholder farmers towards land fragmentation
and consolidation is assessed, the production and production efficiency as well as the
determinants under land fragmentation and consolidation scenarios is evaluated in the
third conceptual framework stance of this research work. Thus, Stochastic Frontier Analysis (SFA) and Data Envelopment Analysis (DEA) models are utilized to estimate
the smallholder farmers production efficiency and a Tobit model helps the researchers to
identify the factors that influence the production efficiency. The conceptual road map of
this PhD thesis is presented in Figure 1. The more meaningful about the work is compare

the different facts which affect the farmland productivity between China and Ethiopia. On that base, you can draw some conclusion and explore the policy implication.

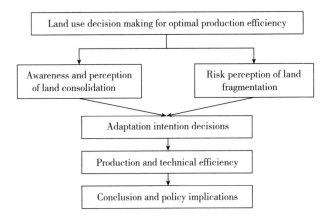

Figure 1   Technology road map

1. 7   Limitation of the study

This thesis work is carried out in two different countries, China and Ethiopia, which have different culture, tradition, language, food, etc. The researcher is motivated to demonstrate and promote the Chinese land consolidation experience to mitigate land fragmentation problems in Ethiopia. However, the researcher faces the following limitations:

(1) Budget constraint is one of the main challenges for the researcher to undertake this thesis work, particularly the transport cost from Chengdu (China) to Addis Ababa

（Ethiopia） was covered by the researcher.

（2） A number of sample units from both study sites are deducted from analysis due to data collection problems（data quality, inappropriate, missing information）.

（3） This research work has a self – report data limitation such as what the people's say on land fragmentation and consolidation through focus group discussion.

（4） Language, weather（winter and summer）, and food are the challenges for the researcher（candidate）during his stay in China.

1. 8   Structure of the thesis

This PhD dissertation comprised of seven chapters. Chapter one presented the general introduction of the study, which include background, statement of the problem, objectives of the study, hypothesis, limitations and the structure of the thesis. Chapter two provides the review of literature related to the land use system, land fragmentation and consolidation in China and Ethiopia. Chapter three showed the general research design and methodology of the thesis. In Chapter four, the awareness, perception and adaptation intention towards land consolidation of Sichuan province smallholder farmers is analyzed. The perspective and adaptive intention to land fragmentation of smallholder farmers in the Central Highlands of Ethiopia is presented in Chapter five. Whereas, Chapter six deals with the smallholder farmers production efficiency under land consolidation and fragmentation scenarios. And finally, Chapter seven provides the general conclusions and policy implications. The dissertation outline is presented in Figure 2.

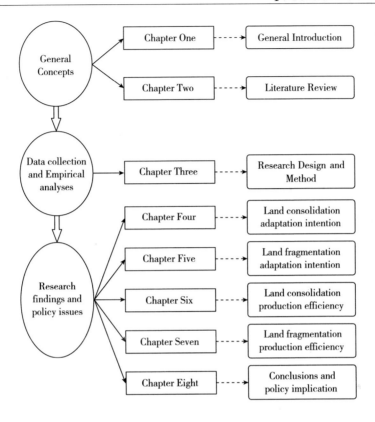

Figure 2　Outline of the dissertation

II. Literature Review

This section need a major revision because in Chinese context, the research should generate the existied researches and present the difference between the exited researches and yours. And the review should be carry on according to the topic/the key words. Obviously, the land tenure system is not the main context of your research.

2.1 Introduction

Land is a public and collective property in China and Ethiopia and administrated by the government thus, individuals and groups as well as private companies have only the land use right in the scope of laws. While, the central idea of this thesis dissertation is the smallholder farmers' engagement in sustainable land use adaptation decisions for optimal agricultural production and efficiency it is very important to review literature of the principles, significance, types and approaches of land use policy, land tenure system, land fragmentation and land consolidation in China and Ethiopia as well as the theories and models of decision making. Therefore, this chapter is organized into five sections: Section 2.2 introduce the land tenure system of pre and post economic reform in China and Ethiopia; Section 2.3 deal with post economic reform land use land cover change in China and Ethiopia; Section 2.4 and Section 2.5 review the definition, advantages and disadvantages land fragmentation and land consolidation respectively; and finally, Section 2.6 provide the theories and models of adaptation decisions.

2. 2   Land tenure systems in China and Ethiopia

Land tenure is defined as the relationship of people's whether individuals or groups with respect to the land (including natural resources such as water and trees) weather legally or customarily (FAO, 2002; Alene Hasan, 2012). Land tenure is a set of rules that determines how land is used, allocated, transferred, possessed, leveraged, and sold or in other ways dispose within the societies or customary in associate of responsibilities and restraints. These rules may be established by the state or by the custom or by the societies and the rights may accrue to individuals, families, communities, or organizations. In simple terms, land tenure systems determine who can use, what resources, for how long, and under what conditions can use. In addition, land tenure is an important multidimensional land use system which bringing into play social, economic, technical, institutional, legal and political aspects (FAO, 2002; Bruce et al., 2010; Alene Hasan, 2012). Therefore, secured access to land is a very crucial factor in achieving food security, eradicating poverty and hunger, resolving disputes violent conflict over access to land, and building long term political, social and economic stability. According to Ma et al. （2013） and Alene Hasan （2012）, the land tenure security is still uncertain in China and Ethiopia.

2. 2. 1 Land use policy and administration in China an overview

In any country, land reform is an intense political process, because the re/distribution and use of real property is under – gird economic system. Modifications of the existing land tenure system and institutional arrangements are bound to create winners and losers, although the net social welfare can be dramatically changed for better or for worse （Riad El – Ghonemy, 1999）. Therefore, land tenure systems and associated legal regimes are not static, but are constantly change depending on the prevailing political ideas and developments of the time. The modern history of China provides an excellent example of this dynamic process.

2. 2. 1. 1 Land tenure pre – 1949

Before 1949 under feudal monarchy, the land tenure system in China comprised of four land use classes and two property rights. The land use classes are landlord, rich, medium and poor peasants and the property use rights are the topsoil （田皮） rights and the subsoil （田骨） rights. The landlord class have had usufruct rights and imminent rights to large tracts of land and earn profits by renting to peasants and paid tax to the government is called subsoil right but they did not have the right actively use the land. The rich and middle class peasants are distinguished largely on the basis of the their land size leases cultivated and paid rent sometimes in kind to landlords called topsoil right. Whereas, the poor class peasants lacked any of their own land and earn a wage by cultivating the lands of the higher classes （Riad El – Ghonemy, 1999; Ho Peter, 2005）.

2. 2. 1. 2 Land tenure between 1949 and 1978

Following the abolition of the feudalistic system and the Communist Party of China

(CPC) comes in power in 1949, land reform was the top priority to return the land from landlords to the poor and landless peasants and tenants. In 1950 China was published a Land Reform Law that abrogated the ownership of land by the landlords and introduced peasants land ownership. The 1950 land reform was one of the largest examples of land expropriation in world history that confiscated 80 to 121 million ha of arable land from the landlords and redistribute to about 75 million landless peasant families as well as to landlord themselves (Ho Peter, 2005). Since 1956 individual land holders reclaimed the land use right put them under the control of collectives, formally institutionalizing collective ownership of rural land but transfer of land use right was subsequently banned and shutting down all markets in land rights (Ding Chengri, 2003; Ho Peter, 2005). Until 1956 China was successfully implemented the small – scale Family Farming System and latter replaced by collective farming system (Bramall, 2004). The collectivization finally developed into an institution called the People's Commune Farming System (production team). Wu (1997) stated that, about 800 million rural people were organized into 52000 Commune Farming System in 1958. The reform liberated productive forces, increased the productivity of agriculture, and laid the basis for the industrialization of China (China. org. cn, September 15, 2009). However, many scholars criticized the Commune Farming System with centrally controlled property rights and a misapplied egalitarian principle of income distribution, resource allocation and movement, the communes hindered the farmers' operational freedom and their enthusiasm for production (Chen and Davis, 1998) and its poor performance and inefficiency land and labor in grain production (Stavis, 1982; Chen, 1994; Wu, 1997).

2. 2. 1. 3   Land tenure system after 1978 reform

At the end of 1970's and the beginning of 1980's, China launched market oriented economic reform and replace the Commune Farming System to Household Responsibility System (HRS). The HRS was first experimented in selected villages of Sichuan (study area) and Anhui provinces and encountered an initial success, and disseminated to agricultural collectives throughout rural China rapidly (Lin, 1992; Tan et al., 2006). The system also acknowledged hundreds of thousands people through quick, massive and equity land re/distribution according to their family size, land quality, and labor force. By 1984, more than 99.5 percent of production teams had adopted the system (Yang, 2004). Moreover, the HRS resolves work incentive problems of the collective system by tightening the link between labor effort and income (Liu et al., 1998). Under this system, land officially remains under collective ownership, land use rights is contracted to the farmers for a short period (one to two years); land could not be transferred between households and it was subject to periodic reallocation among village households to cultivate what they decide by the discretion of the village leader. Reallocation are intended based on the household demographic changes. However, by 1984 the government issued Rural Work Document No. 1 the land use right contract is extended to period of 15 years in order to encourage the farmers investment in land to foster the fertility of the soil and intensive farming. Later in 1998, the central government of China extend the land contract for another 30 years, and disallowed large – scale reallocation of land, limited small – scale readjustments and permitted transfers of land between households (Ping Li, 2003; Lin, 1992; Tan et al., 2006).

At the early stage of the HRS, the agricultural production capacity in the country was significantly improved (Lin, 1992; Tan et al., 2006). However, the other side effect of the HRS was aggravated land fragmentation and production inefficiencies as well as land tenure insecurity. Tan (2005) stated that, after few years of the introduction of the HRS the average number of farm parcels per household was reached more than eight parcels. The land fragmentation becomes more problematic and detrimental implication of private and public investment on agricultural land (such as terracing, planting trees, irrigation and drainage system, rural road network, and agricultural mechanization), sustainable economic growth, social and natural resources development which is a major obstacle to agricultural production growth as well as sustainable rural development in China (Li, 1995; Nguyen et al. , 1996; Wu et al. , 2005; Tan et al. , 2006) . In addition, as the global market economy grew rapidly the HRS cannot compete with the situation because the land ownership in remains at the village/collective organizations and the state (government) .

According to the China's Constitution Article 9 and 10 and Land Resource Management Law, the land resources in the urban region are owned by the state while in rural region the land resources is owned by the collective economic organization according to the laws and regulations, otherwise, they belongs to the state (He Ge, 2012; Benjamin and Brandt, 2002; Li Ling and David Isaac, 1994) . Thus, cities, towns, a large forest and some farmlands are owned under state while rural area, towns which are not governed by the state are owned by rural collective organizations. Therefore, individual households obtained only the land use rights in the scope of the law and they cannot sell and transfer (lease or assign or mortgage) their land use rights to other. Thus, land user has only obtained the land use right (not the land or any resources in or below the land) from land administration department by agreement, tender or auction.

2. 2. 2 An overview of land use policy and administration in Ethiopia

In Ethiopia, land is extremely important and has become a major socioeconomic asset. The agricultural land continues as key for livelihood and financial security as well as profound as people's living standard, wealth and social status, and aspirations indicator of rural areas of Ethiopia. However, due to rapid population growth, land degradation, geography, urbanization and industrial development the agricultural land become a scare resource in the country (USAID, 2004; Belay et al., 2005; ERSS, 2013). In addition, the problem of land tenure insecurity hampers the country economic development throughout the late 19th and 20th centuries. Attempts have been made to modernize land ownership under imperial rules like Emperor Haile Selassie and Marxist regime *Derg* but have mixed results. When the present Ethiopian People Revolutionary Democratic Front (EPRDF) government put in power in 1995 try to improve land tenure security and vest "land is the common property of Nations, Nationalities and Peoples of Ethiopia and shall not be subject to sale or to other means of exchange" (EPRDF, 1995) but it is still insufficient.

2.2.2.1　Pre – 1975 Ethiopian land use policy and administration

Before 1975 the nature of land tenure arrangement was based on feudal system and land was concentrated in the hand of absentee landlords, church, private, state, kinship and other forms. During the imperial Haile Selassie the land tenure types refers mainly under imperial administrative classification which is commonly distinguished as *Rist, Gult, Gebbar, Samon,* and *Madeira* or *Mengist* tenure system (Shimels Tenaw et al., 2009).

Rist is a type of communal land ownership system which all descendants (both male and female) of an individual are entitled to a share and individual had the right to use (usufruct right) a plot of family land. It is hereditary, inalienable, and inviolable and a user of any piece of land could not sell his or her share outside the family and mortgage or bequeath his or her share as a gift, as the land belonged not the individual but to the decent group. This type of tenure affect the minority ethnic group who were tenant farmers. *Gult* tenure system is an ownership right acquired from the monarch or from provincial rulers who were empowered to make land grants. *Gult* owners collect tribute from the farmers and extract labor service as payment in kind from the farmers. *Samon* is a land that the government granted to the Ethiopian Orthodox Church in permanently which estimated 10% ~ 20% of cultivated land of the country. The state owned large tract of agricultural land known as *Mengist* and *Maderia*, which are land registered as government property and land granted mainly to government officials.

Thus, the land tenure system adopted in Ethiopia during the monarchy period was one of the most complex compilation of different land use system in African history. The major problem of the pre – 1975 land tenure in Ethiopia include exploitative occupancy, under concentration and utilization of land and tenure insecurity (Bruce J. W. , et al. , 1994) . There was also problems of institutional inadequacy and the land owned by the absentee landlords were underutilized. Hence, the pre – 1975 land tenure system was considered as the most important obstacles to country economic development in general.

2. 2. 2. 2   Land tenure system between 1975 – 1991

In 1974 popular revolution was held to overthrow the monarchy regime ones for end who dominantly used and benefited land rights and exploited farmer's labor under few feudal landlords and to handover the land to the tiller (Melkamu B. and Shewakena A. , 2010) . Then, in 1974 the Military Junta (*Derg*) assumed power over the state and consequently, adopted the political ideology of socialism, which promote a fair distribution of resource among the citizens and answered the question of the people indirectly by transfer private land ownership to the peoples of Ethiopia and state and allowing individual farmers land use rights.

During this period land was administer by Ministry of Land Reform and Administration (MLRA) through peasant association at the grassroots level and the first land proclamation (Proclamation No. 31/1975) was introduced in the country that declared, the nationalization of all rural land and transferred the landholding and benefits right to the farmers. However, further transfer of land right was highly restricted, because transfer through sale, lease, exchange or mortgage was prohibited, except upon death and only then to wife, husband or children of the deceased (USAID, 2004).

The *Derg* regime also attempts to implement land reform that a new household only get land from their parents by frequent land redistribution which further created land fragmentation problems, constrained new land access, land tenure insecurity, lack of appropriate land use administration and shortage of farm inputs and tools. In general, the *Derg* land policy reform did not result in improving rural livelihoods and the agricultural production growth in the country (Action Aid Ethiopia, 2006).

2.2.2.3 Current land tenure system (since 1994)

Fallowing the dawn fall of *Derg* regime and the current Ethiopian People Revolutionary Democratic Front (EPRDF) government took the power in 1991 they are committed to free market philosophy and made substantive changes in the farmers land use rights while still considered inadequate. By 1994, the first Ethiopian Constitution was drawn with a broad framework for land policy in the country which was approved in 1995 that enshrines the concept of public land ownership and the inalienability of land holdings by sale or exchange. According to Article 40 No. 3, the right to own rural and urban land as well as natural resources belongs only to the state and the peoples. Land is inalienable common property of the nations, nationalities and peoples of Ethiopia and shall not be subjected to sale or to other means of transfer (EPRDF, 1995). Hence, there are no private property right in land in Ethiopia. The landholders are only had usufruct right, they cannot sale nor mortgage their landholdings. In addition, Article 40 No. 4 stated that, Ethiopian peasants have the right to obtain land without payment and guaranteed the protection against eviction from their possession. Thus, the constitution guarantees the rights of peasants free access of land and the right of individual to claim compensation for the improvement and build on the land and shall the right to alienate to bequeath.

EPDRF was introduce the first national land administration and use law was promulgated in July 1997 which was laid down from the fundamental principle of the 1995 Constitution of the country that is referred to as "Rural Land Administration and Use Proclamation No. 89/1997" which provide an umbrella framework for the regional states in enacting rural land administration laws. But regional governments can either issues their own rural land administration laws and land use regulations. This law defines the scope of individual land use right and stated that such right can be leased or bequeathed only (USAID, 2004). However, there was land transfer restriction which the land tenure situation remains ambiguous. In July 2005, the Federal government enacted the "Federal Rural Land Administration and Use Proclamation No. 456/2005" clarified the rural land use rights and obligation and abolished forced land redistribution which was the major cause of land tenure insecurity among rural population and cause land fragmentation. This proclamation reaffirmed the ownership of rural land to the state, but it confers in indefinite tenure rights, rights to property produced on the land, right to inter – generation tenure transfer, right to rent out land, and land lease right to land users for commercial investments. The law makes provision for the registration and certification of land tenure rights and no further land redistribution except under special circumstances.

2.3   Land use land cover change in China and Ethiopia

You should carry on your review according to the main contexts existed. Obviously, land use/land cover change is not the one you should constrate on.

Land use land cover (LULC) change is a process by which human activity transforms the landscape of one land use to other land uses. LULC change is one of the fundamental concerns in environmental change and sustainable development. The wide spread population growth and fast economic developments are the main drivers of LULC change in the past decades which has a negative effect on biophysical process and the climate system (Drealing et al., 2010; Yirsaw et al., 2017). For example, the conversion of land from agricultural production to urban and industrial development is one of the critical processes of change in developing economies undergoing industrialization, urbanization, and globalization (He et al., 2012).

2.3.1 Land use change in China

China is the fourth largest country in the world next to Russia, Canada and the United States that estimated 960 million hectors. The fact that China has been overlooking rapid industrialization and urbanization development in the past three decades and contributing greatly to boost - up the economic growth, but it is also an inevitable for huge land use land cover change. The land use land cover change has been widely seen since the introduction of open market economy in 1978 particularly at the beginning of the new millennium. According to the National Bureau of Statistics (NBS) of China yearbook report, the agricultural land was increased by 37.4% between 1995 and 2000 and keep constant up to 2005 (Figure 1). However, a 6.4% agricultural land reduction has been observed between 2005 and 2010. Yan (2010) also found that, between 2002 and 2010 a total of 3.49 million ha of cultivated land were shifted to new construction land. This showed that about two hundred thousand hectors of arable land were lost annually for new construction. The loss of agricultural land threatens the grain security of the whole country while excessive control of urban expansion can also have adverse

effects on the development of industrialization and urbanization (Li, et al., 2014).
Zhao (2011) also confirmed that China's rapid urbanization has contributed greatly to
economic growth, while it has also led to huge losses of farmland. However, between
2010 to 2015 the agricultural land showed an increment of 14 million ha (10.9%)
(NBS, 2016). In addition, the forest land use was consistently increased between
1995 and 2010 with 9.2% average annual increment. However, between 2010 and
2015 the forest land was decreased by 17.3% (52 million ha). Further, the grass-
lands were also dramatically declined (46%) between 2010 and 2015. This might be
due to the fast industrial and urban expansions. According to He Ge (2012), between
1995 and 2005 the buildup of new industrial/mining and urban areas had increased by
0.9 million ha and 0.45 million ha, respectively.

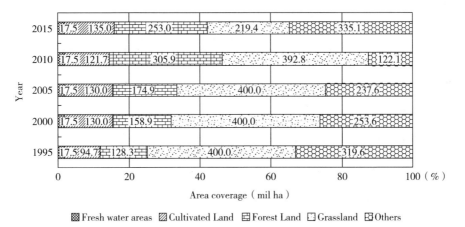

Figure 1　Land use land cover (LULC) change in China 1995 – 2015

Source: NBS.

2.3.2　Land use change in Ethiopia

It is obvious that Ethiopia has facing a serious LULC change problems, mainly as a result of population growth and the need for new agricultural lands, which have contributed to the clearing of forests and other natural land covers. According to data obtained from Food and Agriculture (FAO), the agricultural land use is increasing year on year with an average of 0.286 million ha in the past two decades. While forest and other land covers are declining year on year by 0.286 million ha (Figure 2). Previous studies conducted by Argaw et al. (1999), Ayalew et al. (2005), Tekle and Hedlund (2000), Garedew et al. (2009), and Meshesha et al. (2012) have addressed that, LULC change in Ethiopia accompanying land degradation and soil erosion problems that leading to food insecurity, as well as social and economic problems. Moreover, Tadesse (2001), Zeleke and Hurni (2001) noted that, agricultural productivity is tremendously affected by problems related to LUCC.

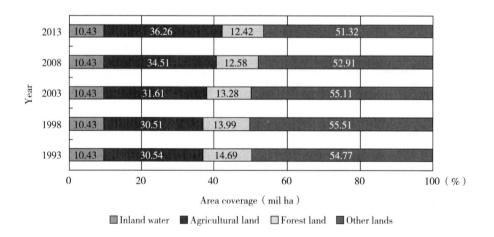

Figure 2 Land use land cover (LULC) change in Ethiopia 1993 – 2013

Source: FAO.

2. 4   Land fragmentation

2. 4. 1   Definitions of land fragmentation

We don't review the definitions. If you want to give out the definitions of the key words, you can list it in the first section to make the reader know that there are some academic words have different means.

Land fragmentation is a common feature across the globe especially in agrarian developing countries. According to McPherson (1982) and King and Burton (1982), land fragmentation defined as the practice of farming a number of spatially dispersed or separated plots of land which are farmed as single unit and owned by the single farmer. Van Dijk (2003) distinguishes four types of land fragmentation: land ownership fragmentation, land use fragmentation, within a farm (internal) fragmentation, and separation of ownership and use. Land ownership fragmentation refers to the number of landowners who use a given piece of land. Land use fragmentation refers to the number of users that are also tenants of the land. The internal fragmentation emphasizes the number of parcels exploited by each user and considers parcel size, shape and distance as the main issues. The separation of ownership and use fragmentation involves the situation where there is a discrepancy between ownership and use. Thus, this PhD thesis mainly focus on internal land fragmentation.

2. 4. 2   Advantages and disadvantages of land fragmentation

You should give the main conclusion of the existed research. I don't think the advantages and disadvantages are the main ideas of the exited research.

Land fragmentation has both positive and negative advantages and the debate about which side outweighs the other seems to be a perpetual one. However, the costs of land fragmentation are quite many compared to its advantages. Many studies indicated that land fragmentation: ①leads to increase traveling time between fields, hence lower labor productivity and higher transport costs for inputs and outputs; ②involves negative external such as reduced scope for irrigation, soil conservation investments and loss of land for boundaries and access routes; ③may also incur farmers to higher costs of supervising workers on each separate farm than when supervision of large farms; ④also involves greater potential for disputes between neighbors on farm boundary; and finally ⑤it is a major obstacle for agricultural production and efficiency (Bentley, 1987; Di Faland consolidationo et al., 2010; Hung et al., 2007; Jabarin and Epplin, 1994; McPherson, 1982; Thomas, 2006; Tan et al., 2008). Hence, to overcome the negative impacts of land fragmentation many countries of Europe (Netherlands, France, Germany, Bulgaria); Africa (Kenya, Tanzania, Rwanda) and Asia (Vietnam, China, Japan) has been implementing and encouraging land consolidation (Blarel et al., 1992; Tan et al., 2006; Thomas, 2006; Hung et al., 2007).

The existence of land fragmentation holdings are regarded as an important feature for less developed agricultural systems (Blarel et al., 1992; Hung et al., 2007; Hristov, 2009). Some literature noted that, it can be an adaptive strategy and under certain circumstances and might have beneficial effects in terms of risk management, crop scheduling, and ecological variety (King and Burton, 1982; Blarel et al., 1992; Tan et al., 2008; Di Faland Consolidationo et al., 2010). For instance, it can facilitate risk management through crop diversification and operating on scattered plots to reduce the risk of total crop loss by flood, drought, fire, frost and other perils, it may enable households spread their own labor over the seasons, and if induced by e-galitarian land redistribution, it may improve food security and equity among farm households (Bentley, 1987; Blarel et al., 1992).

2.4.3 Causes of land fragmentation

The same reason as above, you should revise this section carefully.

The causes of land fragmentation might be different from countries to countries. However, the most common causes of land fragmentation can be grouped into socio – cultural, economic, physio – geographical and institutional (political decision) factors. The socio – cultural factor is the land fragmentation through land inheritance that grant equal access by all the heirs to the assets left behind by the deceased and this principle continues in geometrical progression with each generation that inherits the land (Jabarin and Epplin, 1994; Ram et al., 1999; Niroula and Thapa, 2005; Di Faland Consolidationo et al., 2010). Land fragmentation driven by economic factor is the farmer's desire to expand his farm can buy plots of land that are not adjacent to his property, thus raising further the degree of fragmentation of agricultural land (Simion, 2008). The physio – geographical and operational factors are the fragmentation of the agricultural land damage particularly through the land sliding or slipping, climate conditions and various interventions such as the installation of a fence or the building of railroads, highways and canals that split large land into several plots (Simion, 2008). Finally, the institutional (political decisions) factor is the land fragmentation through land re/distribution and allocation systems.

In line to the pros and cons and regard to the emergence and persistence of land fragmentation Bentley (1987) and Blarel et al. (1992) stated two conventional explanations appeared, namely the *demand – side* explanation and the *supply – side* explanation. The *demand – side* explanation views land fragmentation as a choice variable for farmers in terms of crop diversification and production risk likelihood reduction. Whereas, the *supply – side* explanation treats are an exogenous factors which imposition on farmers resulting for instance population pressure, egalitarian land distribution policy (inheritance) and land scarcity (limited land).

Generally, in China and Ethiopia, land fragmentation is mainly caused by the fair distribution of land to land users according to the soil fertility classes, distance from homestead and agro – ecology on the decisions taken at the local level. This can be explained as supply – side explanation (Tan, 2006; USAID, 2004).

2.4.4 Land fragmentation measurement

There are several land fragmentation indicator parameters and the most common are: farm size, number of plots, plot shape, plot distance from homestead, spatial distribution of the plot, and the size distribution of the fields (King and Burton, 1982). But, there is no standard measurement of land fragmentation and makes difficult to provide precise land fragmentation status of a given farm household compared to others (Bentley, 1987; Hung et al., 2007). Hence, the most common land fragmentation measurements are:

2.4.4.1 Simmons Index (SI)

The SI is originally developed by Simmons (1964) that taking into account the number of parcels and their relative size (a_i). SI is calculate by dividing the square sum of each parcels to the total size square (Eq. 1) and its value ranges between zero and one. Thus, the SI value closer to zero indicates that there is no/less fragmentation and a value closer to one indicated there is high land fragmentation.

$$SI = 1 - \frac{\sum_{i=1}^{n} a_i^2}{(\sum_{i=1}^{n} A)^2} \qquad (2-1)$$

Where: SI is Simmons index of land fragmentation; A is total area of landholding or property; a_i is the land size of the ith parcel.

2. 4. 4. 2　Januszewski Index （K）

Januszewski (1968) also developed another index to measure land fragmentation which the application makes it possible to describe the layout of areas of a single property among its land parcels. The index recommended by Januszewski for measuring of the fragmentation of land is quite similar in nature to the Simmons's index. K is calculate by dividing the square root of the total area of the land property and use by the square root of the sum of the areas of the land parcels (Eq. 2). The K value ranges between zero and one, and a K value closer to 0 indicated that highly fragmented and decrease accordingly.

$$K = \frac{\sqrt{A}}{\sum_{i=1}^{n} \sqrt{a_i}} \qquad (2-2)$$

Where: K is Januszewski index of land fragmentation; A is total area of landholding or property; a_i is the land size of the ith parcel.

2. 4. 4. 3　Parcelization Index （P_i）

The Parcelization index was proposed by Igbozurike (1974) an equation based on a mean size of parcels and a distance covered by a landholder on each consecutive trip to all his parcels (in one journey to and from all his/her parcels) (Eq. 3).

$$P = \frac{\left(\frac{1}{S_i}\right)}{\left(\frac{S_i}{100}\right)} \cdot Dt \qquad (2-3)$$

Where, P is Parcelization index of land fragmentation; S_i is the size of each parcel and Dt is the total round – trip distance covering all parcels.

However, King and Burton (1982) criticized the P index because distance has not been clearly defined by the researcher and is overemphasized, without taking into account the number of parcels.

2.5 Land consolidation

In the 12th century the traditional land consolidation was start implementing in many parts of the world including in China, which mainly regarded as land management approach for rural development due to agriculture has predominant role in the rural area at that time (Wang, 1997; Van Dijk, 2003). However, the modern land consolidation introduced in the late of 19th and early of 20th century and it primarily focused on the creation of competitive agricultural production arrangements by enabling farmers to have larger and better shaped fields rather than fragmented small parcel, including environmental protection, landscape and nature conservation, recreation and renewal of village, developing regional projects and concepts that affect the living and working condition rural area residents apparently to achieve sustainable rural development (FAO, 2003; Vitikainen, 2004). Particularly, land consolidation become a worldwide phenomenon after the World War Ⅱ and carried out in many developed countries of rural Europe, North America, Australia, Japan which are experienced rapid industrialization and urbanization and other developing countries such as Tanzania, Uganda, and Kenya, have a significant impact on agricultural production and sustainable rural development.

2.5.1 Definitions, types, principles and approaches of land consolidation

Many countries have given different definitions to cover the contents of land consolidation depending on the country's objectives. King and Burton (1983) defined land consolidation is a kind of land reform but its objective is different. Land reform is the re/distribution of land in national or regional level to achieve social equity in terms of land ownership, while land consolidation is the redistribution of land in a particular locality aiming to achieve an optimal land tenure structure to facilitate rational agricultural development (King and Burton, 1983). Wu et al. (2005) broadly defined land consolidation as practice to improve land quality that includes: ①expanding of irrigation and drainage system in the areas; ②improving farm plot configuration (plot size, shape and layout) of smaller and irregular shaped plots into larger and regular size and shape through a suitable merging; ③improving farm road systems to provide better access to plots for both workers and machinery; and ④reducing many small, non-contiguous and scattered plots of land. Land consolidation is a set of spatial-planning, legal, organizational, economic and technical measures undertaken for the purpose of improving natural, economic and ecological living and labor conditions in a land territory (Thomas, 2006). Vladan Dokic and Stevan Marosan (2008) also noted land consolidation encompasses the planning and renewal of rural settlements and accordingly, is a strong driving force for overall development of settlements (rural development) and environmental protection. Thus, the general objectives of land consolidation are to improving the production and working conditions in agriculture and forestry as well as promoting the general use and development of land and rural areas by rearrangement of agricultural land (FAO, 2003; Thomas, 2005). These objectives are pursued by land exchanges between real estate generally without changes of ownership or users of land. In addition to actual land exchanges improvement of the road and drainage network, building, landscaping, environmental management and conservation projects, and other functions may be implement. Land consolidation is one of the most important elements for helping to solve the rural structural problems in agriculture and agricultural production and many international advisers called land consolidation as a "secret weapon" for economic growth and share the wealth (Thomas, 2006).

According to FAO (2003), there are four approaches and five types and principles of land consolidation. The five types and principles of land consolidation are summarized in Figure 3. The four approaches of land consolidation are:

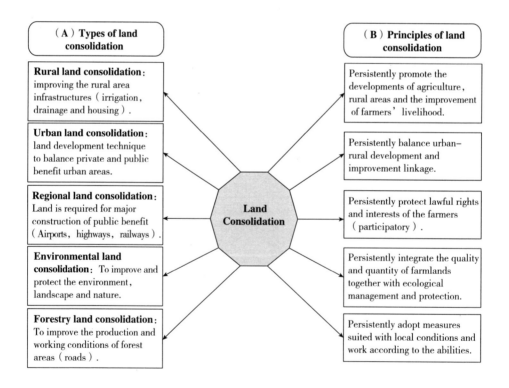

Figure 3   The types and principles of land consolidation

Source: FAO, 2003.

(1) Comprehensive land consolidation: is the most effective and appropriate land consolidation approach to integrate rural development with a view of improving the production and working conditions in agriculture and forestry as well as promoting the general use and development of land. It re – arrange and consolidated scattered and uneconomically shaped parcels to meet modern managerial requirements and reshape to obtain units of a more favorable location, shape and size, and provide road, irrigation, and other physical rural infrastructures. It is the most expensive land consolidation approach compare to other approaches.

(2) Simplified land consolidation: can be implemented to eliminate or minimize the detrimental impacts on the agricultural structure caused by public request to land use such as transport planning, communal land use planning, water management planning or planning concerning nature protection and landscape. It can also optimizes conditions in the agricultural sector through the reallocation or exchange of parcels and the provision of additional lands from land banks. These simplified projects are often combined with the rehabilitation of infrastructure through public projects and sometimes the provision of minor facilities but they do not include the construction of major public works although they can provide the framework for their construction at a later stage.

(3) Voluntary (grouped) land consolidation: is implemented only aims to reduce the fragmentation and to merge the scattered and uneconomically shaped parcels of farms. It is the simplest, fastest and inexpensive land consolidation measure. Parcels of two or more owners are exchanged and merged their land with full agreement. Voluntary land consolidation projects tend to be small and are best suited to address minor and localized problems.

(4) Individual land consolidation: is individual consolidation of holdings can take place on an informal and sporadic basis. The state or local government is not directly in-

volved so these initiatives do not include the provision of public facilities. However, the government can play a significant role in encouraging consolidations that improve agriculture by promoting policies such as joint land – use agreements, leasing and retirement schemes. Generally, the difference between the above land consolidation approaches is due to the legal aspects and the procedures they follow.

2. 5. 2   Advantages and disadvantages of land consolidation

Land consolidation like other land development and management programs it has its own advantages and limitations. The most common advantages and disadvantages are presented in Table 1.

Table 1   Advantages and disadvantages of land consolidation

Advantages	Disadvantages
It increase the rational agricultural development (productivity, mechanization) .	It can affect the nature of the ecosystem and biodiversity.
It improve natural resource management, planning and utilization.	It can reduce crop diversification and increase the crop failure risk.
It restructure land tenure security and can solve public – private conflicts.	It may displace community from their original place.
It resolve the urban – rural income inequality gaps.	It can create soil erosion by wind because there is no plant for windbreak.
It can facilitate public and private investment in land (road, irrigation, drainage, inputs) .	It may destroy farm boundary and hedgerow which are used as fencing and erosion control.
It can improve land administration system and land information.	It may cause environmental pollution due to construction work.
It support the sociopolitical stability in rural areas. It can create tidy and clean village.	It requires high initial investment especially for comprehensive land consolidation approach.

Source: FAO (2003) and Demetriou (2014) .

2. 5. 3　Land consolidation in China

In China, the traditional land consolidation began in 1066 (Wang, 1997) while the modern land consolidation was start implementing since the establishment of Land Consolidation and Rehabilitation Center (LCRC) in 1998 (Wang et al. , 2014). China motivated to implement land consolidation is to overcome the rural agricultural production challenges such as to achieve food security and sustain rural development.

Since the establishment of LCRC, China launch the National Land Consolidation Plan and give more attention by incorporating in the national Five Year Strategic Plan (FYSP). According to Wang et al. (2014) during the first decade of the land consolidation project implementation and the 10th and 11th FYSP achievement 2. 8 million ha of farmland was supplied and 13. 3 million ha farmland with high and stable productivity was fully built through carrying out land consolidation. Liu et al. (2013) also reported that 6. 99 million ha to 9. 92 million ha rural land consolidation potential exist within four different urbanization scenarios. During the 12th FYSP (2011 to 2015) China had plan to construct 26. 67 million ha high quality farmland to ensure national grain security; consolidate 0. 3 million ha rural residential land to rationalizing rural settlement; supply 2. 64 million ha of new cultivated land by consolidation 1. 19 million ha from agricultural land; and reclaim 0. 4 million ha damaged land and 1. 05 million ha from unused land suitable for cultivation (Li et al. , 2014). Still there is a long way ahead for land consolidation plan expected during the 13th FYSP (2016 to 2020) to achieve food security and to sustain rural development socially, economically and environmentally (Huang et al. , 2011).

2. 5. 4　Land consolidation in Ethiopia

In recent years the Ethiopian government attempts to shift from small – scale subsistence farming to large – scale mechanize farming system to modernize the agricultural system and increase the grain production as well as to meet self – food sufficiency and economic growth. In Ethiopia land consolidation is not started yet as developmental program, however, the government encouraged a voluntary bases land consolidation. In Ethiopia rich farmers try to enlarge their farm size through rent – in and share – in approaches from their neighbor poor farmers. Haile et al. (2005) and Segers et al. (2010) reported that farmers who have formal user rights on plots that are far from their homestead but near other farmer's home have exchanged plots on voluntary bases.

2.6   Adaptation decision theories and models

Decision making is a cognitive process in the identifying and selection of alternatives of problem solving activities for optimal or at least satisfactory results. Smallholder farmers have diverse activities and are highly variable in decision making due to their various aspects of farming system, environmental and living conditions. Developing, testing and implementing innovative decision making tools regarding to the smallholder farmer farming system, environmental and living conditions to enhance their decision capabilities for optimal production and efficiency are very important.

The smallholder farmers decision making on agricultural technologies, climate change and sustainable land management adaptation intentions has attract the interest of many scholars and researchers. Several theories and models have been developed to address the human complex behavior of judgment uncertainty. Ajzen (1991) develop the Theory of Planned Behavior (TPB) which is the extension of Theory of Reasoned Action (TRA) (Ajzen and Fishbein, 1980) . Both models are based on the premise that individuals make logical, reasoned decisions to engage or not engaged in specific behaviors by evaluating the available information. The performance of a behavior is determined by predicting an individual's intention to engage (perform) or not engage (not perform) in a particular behavior. TPB helps to understand how people change and deliberate their adaptation intention behavior. Davies (1989) also proposed Technology Acceptance Model (TAM) extensions of Ajzen and Fishbein's TRA which most widely applied model of users' acceptance and usage of technology. TAM has been widely criticized despite its frequent use. Chuttur (2009) said that, TAM has lack of sufficient rigor, limited explanatory and predictive power, triviality, and lack of any practical value.

In China and Ethiopia there is lack of evidence on smallholder farmers adaptation decisions towards land consolidation and land fragmentation, particularly in Sichuan province and Amhara region (the Central Highlands of Ethiopia) . Thus, this PhD thesis adopted the TPB model to investigate the smallholder farmers' engagement in land consolidation and land fragmentation adaptation decisions for optimal production efficiency.

As a rule, you should generate the reviews to show the highlights of your research. And this is very necessary.

Ⅲ. Research Design and Methods

3. 1   Introduction

This chapter presents the research methods used to test the hypothesis and conceptual framework of the study in order to achieve the research objectives. It addresses the study areas characteristics, the data collection and sampling techniques used, and the overall research design that lies behind the selection of specific psychological and econometric models and frameworks. Structural Equation Modeling (SEM) is used as a major analytic tool for the smallholder farmers attitude and perception in response to land fragmentation and land consolidation adaptation intentions for optimal production efficiency. The Stochastic Frontier Analysis (SFA) and Data Envelopment Analysis is used to investigate the smallholder farmers production efficiency level under land fragmentation and land consolidation scenarios. While, the Tobit regression model applied to investigate factors influencing the production efficiency of smallholder farmers in China and Ethiopia. It seems the conceptual frame and the following three models (three aspects) is not the same things. That means it is difficult to read the relatives between the conceptual frame and the three models. You should make them more specific. And I am afraid it is too short.

3. 2　Description of the study areas

3. 2. 1　Sichuan province, China

Sichuan province is located in the upper reaches of the Yangtze River Valley in the Southwest of China and situated at 30°08′00″ N latitude and 102°56′00″ E longitude. Sichuan province consists of 21 prefecture level divisions and 181 counties and has a varieties of land forms, including plains (7.8%), hills (10.1%), plateaus or mountains (32.1%), mountainous regions (49.4%), water (0.6%). The average elevation of 2000 to 3500 meter above sea level (m. a. s. l). Sichuan is the fifth largest province in China covers 48.61 million ha area with 35% of forest land, 42% grassland, 20% of agricultural land (NBS, 2016). Due to great differences in terrain, the climate of the province is highly variable. According to Koppen's climate classification the province has strong monsoonal and humid subtropical climate with long, hot, humid summers and short, mild to cool, dry and cloudy winters. The mean annual precipitation of Sichuan province is 1050 mm and the average temperatures ranges from 7℃ to 26℃ (SBS, 2015). The province consists of 19 soil types and yellow earth, purple soil, paddy soil, red soil, limestone soils, and alluvial soils are the major soils. Rice (*Oryza sativa*), wheat (*Tritcum*), maize (*Zea mays*) and sweet potato (*Ipomoea batatas*) are the major staple food crops and peanut (*Arachis hypogaea*), cotton (*Gossypium arboretum*), tobacco (*Nicotiana*) and tea (*Camellia sinensis*) are the most cash (economic) crops in Sichuan province.

3. 2. 2   Amhara region, Ethiopia

Amhara region is one of the nine ethnic divisions of Ethiopia, which consists of eleven administrative zones and 105 *Woredas* (counties). The largest inland water body and the highest mountain are found in the region called Lake Tana (Blue Nile River) and Ras – Dashan, respectively. Amhara region is located in the north western and north central part of Ethiopia and positioned at 11°39′39″ N latitude and 37°57′28″ E longitude. The region covers an estimated area of 170752 square kilometers. Topographically the region is divided into the highlands (above 1500 m. a. s. l) and the lowlands (altitude between 500 to 1500 m. a. s. l). The highlands are comprise the largest part of the northern and eastern parts of the region and the lowland part covers mainly the western and eastern parts. Due to great differences in topography, the region consists of three agro – climatic zones *Kolla* (31%), *Woyna dega* (44%) and *Dega* (25%). The annual mean temperature for most parts of the region lies between 15℃ to 21℃. The region receives the highest percentage of the total rainfall in the country (80%). Amhara region consists of 15 soil types and the major soils are leptosols (52%), verisols (19%) and cambisols (10%). 85% populations of the region is actively engaged in small – scale agriculture. Teff (*Eragrostis tef*), barley (*Hordeum vulgare*), wheat (*Triticum*), sorghum (*Sorghum bicolor*) and maize (*Zea mays*) are the major crops and cotton (*Gossypium hirsutum*), sesame (*Sesamum indicum*), sunflower (*Helianthus annuus*), and sugarcane (*Saccharum officinarum*) are the main cash crops.

The selection of the study areas were elaborated on the basis of a wide desk research review as well as qualitative discussion with researchers of Sichuan Agricultural University (SAU) and Debre Birhan Agricultural Research Center (DBARC) for Sichuan province and Amhara region target groups, respectively. The Sichuan province targeted areas were selected based on their successful Rural Land Consolidation (RLC) program that implemented in partner – based and participatory basis while the Amhara region were based on their higher degree of land fragmentation.

3.3 Data collection and sampling methods

This academic PhD research was carried out in three purposely selected districts from each study province/region. Neijiang, Dujiangyan and Ya'an districts were selected from Sichuan province based on their successful land consolidation programs and Debre Birhan, Efratana Gidim and Moretina Jiru districts from Amhara region based on their land fragmentation levels. This enables the researcher to identify the smallholder farmers' adaptation decisions to land consolidation and land fragmentation for optimal production efficiency in both study areas. Thus, farm household questionnaires were prepared to collect qualitative and quantitative primary data from both countries which the original English version questionnaires was translated into Simplified Chinese and Amharic version for Sichuan and Amhara region study areas, respectively. The farm household questionnaire has consists of three parts: (a) semi – structured questions for collecting information about the socioeconomic conditions of the farm households; (b) a farm household technology input used and production systems questions; and finally；（c） a structural equation modeling questions to collect the farm household adaptation decision towards land consolidation and land fragmentation. A simple random sampling technique was used to collect the empirical cross – section data by means of a face – to – face interview. The researcher tries to including different social class, such as age（young, middle and aged farmers）, gender（male headed and female headed households）, education status, and wealth status（rich, moderate and poor farmers） by agricultural extension agents of the selected counties.

3. 4　Econometric models and frameworks

Based on the viewpoint of sustainable land use management this PhD research work constructs an analytic framework to test the hypothesis and theoretical models. In order to explore the formulation of smallholder farmers' engagement in land fragmentation and consolidation adaptation intention and their production efficiency, the Structural Equation Modeling（SEM）, Data Envelopment Analysis（DEA） and Stochastic Frontier Analysis（SFA） were chosen as econometric models to test the research hypotheses. it seems you referred to the models above. it needn't appear here again.

3. 4. 1　Structural Equation Modeling（SEM）

Joreskog（1977） was introduced a flexible and powerful Structural Equation Modeling（SEM） which is the extension of General Linear Model（GLM） that encompasses such diverse statistical techniques as path analysis, confirmatory factor analysis, causal modeling with latent variables, and even analysis of variance and multiple linear regression that enable the researchers to test a set of regression equation simultaneously. Like other statistical tools SEM has many advantages such as: it bridges the gaps between the theory (which is in terms of latent variables in the first place) and the empiric (which is in terms of observed variables); its measurement and confirmatory factor analysis models can be used to purge errors, making estimated relationships among latent variables less contaminated by measurement error; it has the ability to fit non – standard models, including flexible handling of longitudinal data, databases with auto – correlated error structures (time series analysis), and databases with non – normally distributed variables and incomplete data; it provides the overall tests of model fit and individual parameter estimate tests including the regression coefficients, means, and variances may be compared simultaneously, even across multiple between subject groups; and it reduces the model multicollinearity problem (Folmer et al. , 2010) .

SEM allows handling of observed and latent variables and their relationships within an integrated framework (Joreskog and Sorbom, 2001) . Observed (manifest) variables are indicators (items) that directly measured by the researchers while the latent (unobserved) variables are refers to phenomenon that are supposed to exist but not directly measured and they can be inferred by means of correspondence statements that relate it to a set of observed variables (indicators) . The relationship among the observed (manifest) and unobserved (latent) variables can be represented by path diagram (Figure 1) . In the path diagram the latent variables are represented by oval or circle shapes while the square or rectangle shapes are representing the measured (observed) variables. Further, residuals (errors) are always considered as unobserved items and represented by oval or circle shapes. Thus, in SEM, the independent variables are assumed to be measured without error are called exogenous or upstream variables while the dependent or mediating variables are called endogenous or downstream variables.

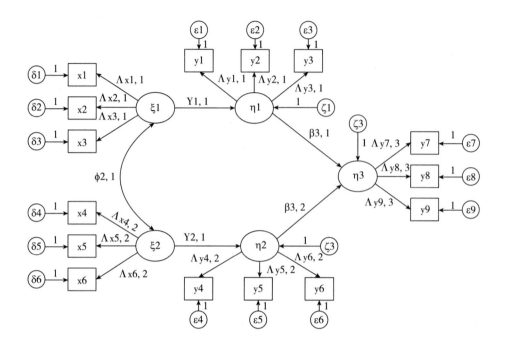

Figure 1   Structural Equation Modeling path diagram

The structural equation model is generally represented by a system of linear equations that consists of two sub – models, the measurement model and the structural model. The measurement model reflects the relationship between the latent variables and their observed indicators. In other words, it specifies how measured variables represent a latent construct that is not measured directly. While, the structural model represents the relationships between the latent exogenous and latent endogenous variables as well as the relationships among the latent endogenous variables (Hair et al. , 2010) . The structural model develops the advantage of path analysis, which can reflect the structural relationship between latent variables, calculate the direct effect between latent variables, deduce the indirect effect and total effect, and express the intermediary role, so as to represent the causal relationship between latent variables.

Structural equation modeling incorporates several different approaches or frameworks to representing these models. However, the general well − known framework of structural equation model by Joreskog, (1977) can be represented by three matrix equations as:

$$X_{(q\times1)} = \Lambda_{x(q\times n)} \times \xi_{(n\times1)} + \delta_{(q\times1)} \tag{3-1}$$

$$Y_{(p\times1)} = \Lambda_{y(p\times m)} \times \eta_{(m\times1)} + \varepsilon_{(p\times1)} \tag{3-2}$$

$$\eta_{(m\times1)} = B_{(m\times m)} \times \eta_{(m\times1)} + \Gamma_{(m\times n)} \times \xi_{(n\times1)} + \zeta_{(m\times1)} \tag{3-3}$$

The first equation represents the measurement model of exogenous observation variables; the second equation represents the measurement model of endogenous observation variables; and the third equation represents the structural model between endogenous latent variables. $X_{(q\times1)}$ and $Y_{(p\times1)}$ are represent the exogenous observation variable and the endogenous observed variable matrix, respectively. $\xi_{(n\times1)}$ and $\eta_{(m\times1)}$ indicates the exogenous latent variable matrix and the endogenous latent variable matrix, respectively. $\Lambda_{x(q\times n)}^{\cdot}$ denotes the exogenous the factor loading matrix of observed variables on exogenous latent variables and $\Lambda_{y(p\times m)}$ denotes the factor loading matrix of endogenous latent variables on endogenous latent variables. $\delta_{(q\times1)}$ denotes the measurement error matrix of exogenous observed variables and $\varepsilon_{(p\times1)}$ represents the measurement error matrix of the endogenous observed variables. $B_{(m\times m)}$ represents the path coefficient matrix between the endogenous latent variables, $\Gamma_{(m\times n)}$ represents the ratio of the exogenous latent variables to the corresponding endogenous of the latent variables, and $\zeta_{(p\times1)}$ denotes the measurement error matrix of the endogenous latent variables. The "p, q, m and n" are the number of endogenous observed variables, the number of exogenous observed variables, the number of endogenous latent variables and the number of exogenous latent variables, respectively. SEM can be graphically represented as:

Therefore, taking the advantages of Theory of Planed Behavior (TPB) this PhD research work develops two broad conceptual frameworks that incorporated in the SEM. The first research framework is conceptualized to examine the Sichuan smallholder farmers' engagement in land consolidation adaptation intentions which answer the research questions: to what extent the social networks and media contribute in the development of smallholder farmers' awareness and perception of land consolidation as well as adaptation intentions; and how much the local farmers perception and awareness of land consolidation influence their adaptation intentions. These issues and causality relationship between the variables have been briefly discussed in Chapter 4. The second conceptual framework of this research work is how much the Amhara region smallholder farmers intended to adopt the land fragmentation problems in order to achieve optimal agricultural productions (Chapter 5). Thus, to ascertain the second framework: how the local farmers are perceived the land fragmentation risks, what adaptation measures are using to cope land fragmentation; who is influencing their adaptation and intentions towards land fragmentation; and does social incentives affect the intention of local farmers. In addition, the impact of land fragmentation level, crop diversity, farmland size and number of plots on the adaptation intention were also tested.

3.4.2　Data preparation and diagnostic

Prior to the complex multivariate analysis of SEM the collected raw data first has to be checked the data adequacy and consistency measurement, validity, reliability and correlation matrix using KMO test, Cronbach's alpha (α), factor loading (λ), the average variance extracted (AVE), square root of AVE, and composite reliability (CR).

Kaiser – Meyer – Olkin (*KMO*) tests is a measure how the constructed variable data are suited for factor analysis and measures sampling adequacy for each variable in the model as well as for the complete model. KMO indicates the proportion of variance in the variables that might be caused by underlying factors. According to the rule of thumb, the KMO values range between 0 and 1. Thus, KMO value 0. 8 and above indicate the sampling is adequate while 0. 6 and lower KMO value is inadequate (Kaiser, 1974; Hair et al. , 2010) . KMO mathematically expressed as:

$$KMO_j = \frac{\sum_{i \neq j} r_{ij}^2}{\sum_{i \neq j} r_{ij}^2 + \sum_{i \neq j} u} \qquad (3-4)$$

Where: $R = [r_{ij}]$ is the correlation matrix, and $U = [u_{ij}]$ is the partial co – variance matrix.

Cronbach's Alpha (α): It is an index to test the reliability and internal consistency associated with the underlying construct being measured, that is how closely related a set of items are as a group. The Cronbach's alpha value ranges between 0 and 1, as a rule of thumb, a value 0. 70 or higher indicated that the data is reliable and internally consistent (Hair et al. , 2010) .

$$\alpha = \frac{N \cdot \bar{c}}{\bar{v} + (N - 1) \cdot \bar{c}} \qquad (3-5)$$

Where: N is the number of item, c – bar is the average inter – item co – variance among the items, and v – bar is the average variance.

Factor Loading (λ): it indicates to what extent a factor explains a variable in the factor analysis. Factor loading is basically the correlation coefficient for the variable and factor. The loading can range from – 1 to 1 and a λ close to – 1 or 1 indicate that the factors are strongly affects the variable and loading close to zero indicate that the factor has a weak effect on the variable. As a rule of thumb, a λ value 0. 5 or higher factor loading represents that the factor extracts sufficient variance from that variable (Hair et al. , 2010) .

Composite reliability (*CR*) *and Average Variance Extracted* (*AVE*) are used to measure the convergent and discriminate validity of each construct variables. The convergent and discriminant validity examine the extent to which measures of a latent variable shared their variance and how they are different from others. Thus, AVE measures the level of variance captured by a construct versus the level due to measurement error and its value above 0. 7 considered very good and the level of 0. 5 is acceptable. CR is a less biased estimate of reliability than Cronbach's Alpha, and its acceptable value is 0. 7 and above. CR and AVE cab be mathematically expressed as:

$$CR = \frac{(\sum \lambda_i)^2}{(\sum \lambda_i)^2 + (\sum \varepsilon_i)} \; ; \; \varepsilon_i = 1 - \lambda_i^2 \qquad (3-6)$$

Whereby, λ (lambda) is the standardized factor loading of the ith item (indicator) and ε is the respective error variance of the ith item.

$$AVE = \frac{\sum_{i=1}^{N} L_i^2}{N} \qquad (3-7)$$

Where, L is the square of standard factor loading, and N is the number of factor loadings (items) .

After the model reliability and validity checking the structural model estimation preceded the interpretation of path coefficients of structural equation fit (R^2) was computed. The item R – square value is the percent of the variance of the ith item explained by the latent variable. It is estimated as:

$$R^2 = \lambda_i^2 = 1 - \varepsilon_i \qquad (3-8)$$

3. 4. 3   Confirmatory Factor Analysis (CFA)

Confirmatory factor analysis (CFA) is a powerful multivariate statistical procedure that is used to test how well the measured variables represent the number of constructs and used to confirm or reject the measurement theory. Confirmatory factor analysis (CFA) and exploratory factor analysis (EFA) are similar techniques, but EFA data is simply explored and provides information about the numbers of factors required to represent the data. In EFA, all measured variables are related to every latent variable but in CFA the researcher can specify the number of factors required in the data and which measured variable is related to which latent variable.

Hence, the CR, AVE, MSV, Correlation matrix and SQR − AVE results of the observed items and their associate construct variables are in an acceptable range and support to develop the model, the next step is determining the measurement model and structural model factor analysis using CFA and checked by Goodness − of − Fit (GOF) index. For the GOF, there are several criteria grouped into Chi − square index, absolute fit index, incremental fit index and parsimony fit index. Chi − square index is the most popular index to assess the overall goodness of fit of the model. It includes Chi − square (CMIN) (χ^2), degree of freedom (df) and Normed Chi − square (CMIN/df). Absolute fit index indicate the extent to which the full structural equation model provides an acceptable fit to the data without using an alternative model as a base for comparison (Hair et al. , 2010). Absolute fit index include Goodness of Fit Index (GFI), Root Mean Square Error Approximation (RMSEA), Root Mean Square Residual (RMR), and Standardized Root Mean Square Residual (SRMR). Incremental index assess how well the estimated model fits relative to some alternative baseline models (Hair et al. , 2010). The most baseline model assumed all observed variables are uncorrelated. They includes Normed Fit Index (NFI), Tucker Lewis Index (TLI), Comparative Fit Index (CFI) and Relative Non − centrality Index (RNI). Whereas, the parsimony fit index provide information about which model is best considering its fit relative to its complexity (Hair et al. , 2010). They includes Adjusted Goodness of Fit Index (AGFI), P – CLOSE and Parsimony Normed Fit Index (PNFI). However, it is not practical to apply all cutoff values of the GOF indexes for assessing a single model because there is no single "magic" value always distinguishes the good models form bad models (Hair et al. , 2010).

3. 5 Production efficiency estimations

There are two most common techniques being used in the measurement of efficiency, the parametric or Stochastic Frontier Approach (SFA) and the non – parametric or Data Envelopment Analysis (DEA) (Coelli, 1995). A parametric frontier has a precise mathematical form whereas a non – parametric approach formed using a certain assumptions about the nature of the technologies. Both SFA and DEA approaches are derived from the methods of measuring efficiency introduced by Farrell (1957) who suggested measuring the efficiency of a firm relative to an empirical production frontier. Many studies noted that, there is no clear evidence that indicate the best efficiency estimation technique (Olsen et al. , 1996; Dhungana et al. , 2004). Thus, researchers can safely choose any technique as long as there is no significant difference between the estimate results (Thaim et al. , 2001; Witkin, 2013). In this study we have used both techniques to estimate the smallholder farmer's production efficiency level in Sichuan province and the Central Highlands of Ethiopia.

3.5.1 Stochastic Frontier Analysis (SFA)

SFA was originally developed by Aigner et al. (1977) which provide a convenient

framework for conducting hypothesis testing since it uses statistical techniques to estimate the parameters and it imposes specific assumptions on both the functional form of
the frontier and the distribution of the error term. Differently from non – parametric approach that assume deterministic frontiers, SFA allows for deviations from the frontier
whose error can be decomposed for adequate distinction between technical efficiency and
random shocks. The SFA model can be estimated as:

$$y_i = f(x_i;\ \beta) + \varepsilon_i \quad \varepsilon_i = v_i - u_i \tag{3-9}$$

Where, Y_i is the output quantity of the ith farmers, X_i is the input parameters used
of the ith farmer. β is a parameter to be estimated. The V_i is the random variable which is
assumed to be independent and identically distributed (iid) N $(0,\ \sigma_v^2)$ and U_i is a
non – negative random variable represents the inefficiency assumed to be distributed independently V_i and $U_i \geqslant 0$.

3. 5. 2　Data Envelopment Analysis (DEA)

DEA uses linear programming (LP) methodology for evaluating the relative efficiency of decision – making units (DMUs) with multiple inputs and multiple outputs
Charnes et al. (1978). The DEA does not require any functional form or distribution
type and less sensitive to unspecific relative to SFA.

Assume that a farm household DMU_i use a vector of k discretionary inputs to produce a vector of r outputs. We represent the individual net inputs and outputs for DMU_i
as x_{ij} and y_{ip} respectively. The output efficiency of DMU_0 (where DMU_0 is the unit in the
collection of DMU_i (i =1, 2, 3, $\cdots$, n) which is being assessed) is $1/\theta_0^*$ where θ_0^*
is the optimal value of θ_0 and the DEA linear programming (LP) can be estimated as:

$$\max(\theta_0 + \varepsilon(\sum_{j=1}^{k} r_j^- + \sum_{p=1}^{r} r_p^+)) \tag{3-10}$$

Subjected to:

$$\sum_{i=1}^{n} x_{ij}\lambda_i = x_{j0} - r_j^- \quad (j = 1, 2, \cdots, k)$$

$$\sum_{i=1}^{n} y_{ip}\lambda_i = \theta_0 y_{p0} + r_p^+ \quad (p = 1, 2, \cdots, r)$$

Where, $_i$, r_j^-, $r_p^+ \geq 0$, i, j, p, θ_0 unconstrained; y_{ip} is the level of output r and x_{ij} the level of input k for i^{th} DMU, and ε is a vanish small positive number (Coelli, 1995).

Farrell (1957) categorized the efficiency measurement into three: Technical Efficiency (TE), Allocative Efficiency (AE), and Economic Efficiency (EE). The technical efficiency refers to the ability of farm household DMUs to minimize input use while maintaining a given output level or the ability to maximize output production while fixing the amount of inputs uses. Whereas, allocative efficiency denotes to the ability of farm household DMUs to utilize minimum input costs to produce a given level of outputs. Economic efficiency is the product of both TE and AE (Farrell, 1957; Coelli, 1995). Thus, a farm household DMU is economically efficient if it is technically and allocatively efficient.

The mathematical equations of input – oriented VRS – DEA model of TE of DMUs:

$$TE_i = \min_{\lambda_i \theta_i,} \theta_i \qquad (3-11)$$

Subjected to:

$$\sum_{i=1}^{n} \lambda_i x_{ik} - \theta_i x_{ik} \leq 0,$$

$$\sum_{i=1}^{n} \lambda_i y_{ik} - \theta_i y_{ir} \geq 0,$$

$$\sum_{i=1}^{n} \lambda_i = 0,$$

$$\lambda_i \geq 0$$

Where i is non – negative vector weight (constants) which defines the linear combination of the peers of the ith DMU. θ_i is a scalar $\leqslant 1$ that defines the TE of DMU$_i$, with a value of 1 indicating a technically efficient and a value less than 1 indicating a technically inefficient (Coelli, 1995).

Similarly, the LP input – oriented VRS – DEA model of EE of DMUs a cost minimization is computed as:

$$EE_i = \min_{\lambda_i x_i^*}, \sum_{i=1}^{n} c_{ik} x_{ik}^* \qquad (3-12)$$

Subjected to:

$$\sum_{i=1}^{n} \lambda_i x_{ik} - \theta_i x_{ik}^* \leqslant 0,$$

$$\sum_{i=1}^{n} \lambda_i y_{ir} - \theta_i y_{ir}^* \geqslant 0,$$

$$\sum_{i=1}^{n} \lambda_i = 0,$$

$$\lambda_i \geqslant 0$$

Where c_{ik} is a transpose vector of the input costs of the ith DMU and X_{ik}^* is the cost – minimizing vector of input k for the ith DMU. All the other variables are as previously defined. EE can be represented by the product of TE and AE (Farrell, 1957).

However, the *Max* DEA statistical package cannot directly provide the allocative efficiency (AE) of the individual DMUs. Thus, AE can be calculated as:

$$AE_i = \frac{EE_i}{TE_i} \qquad (3-13)$$

3.5.3 Tobit Model

Tobit regression model describes the relationship between non – negative dependent variable (Y_i) and an independent variable (X_i) (Tobin, 1958). The model supposes that the un – observable latent variable Y_i^* is linearly depends on a X_i via parameter (vector), β which determines the relationship between the independent variable (vector) X_i and the latent variable Y_i^*. In addition, there is a normally distributed error term ε_i to capture random influences on this relationship which assumed to be independently distributed as truncation at zero of the N $(0, \sigma^2)$ distribution. The Tobit model is mathematically presented in equation 17.

$$E(y_i^* | X) = x_i'\beta \qquad\qquad (3-14)$$

$$y_i^* = \beta_0 + \sum \beta_j X_i + \varepsilon_i$$

$$y_i = \begin{cases} y_i^* & if \begin{array}{l} y_i^* > 0 \\ y_i^* = 0 \end{array} \\ 0 \end{cases}$$

As the efficiency score derived from the SFA and DEA ranges between zero and one, this study employed a censored Tobit regression model to examine the potential determinants of smallholder farmer's production inefficiency using maximum likelihood estimate (MLE).

IV. Land Consolidation Adaptation Intention in China: The Case of Sichuan Smallholder Farmers

4. 1　Introduction

Land consolidation is an effective land management planning and practice to con-figure spatially and uneconomically scattered agricultural lands; solve farm infrastruc-ture problems (irrigation and drainage system and road networks); improve the nature, economic and environmental conditions of rural settlements in order to achieve sustain-able agricultural production and rural development (FAO, 2003; Thomas, 2005).

In China, traditional land consolidation was practiced in the early of the 11th cen-tury (Wang, 1997). However, the modern land consolidation was begun during the establishment of Land Consolidation and Rehabilitation Center (LCRC) in let – 1990. The Chinese central government launched the "National Land Consolidation Programs" and incorporating in the National Five Year Strategic Plan (FYSP) of the country. Since then China investing large amount of manpower, material and financial resources and achieving a remarkable result in reclaiming poor quality soils into medium and high – quality soils; small and uneconomically fragment parcels change to larger and better shape farms, installations of agricultural infrastructures such as irrigation and drainage system, road network; in many land consolidation project areas of the country, particularly in rural areas of Sichuan province.

According to Wang et al. (2014) during the first decade (2000 – 2010) of land consolidation program implementation and 10th and 11th FYSP achievement, 2. 8 million hectares of farmland are supplied and 13. 3 million hectares farmland is reclaimed with high quality and stable productivity was carrying out through land consolidation program. During the 12th FYSP (2011 – 2015) China had planned to consolidate 26. 67 million hectares high – quality farmland to ensure national grain security; to build 0. 3 million hectares of rural residential land to rationalizing rural settlement; to supply 2. 64 million hectares new cultivated land by consolidation of 1. 19 million hectares of agricultural lands; and to reclaim 0. 4 and 1. 05 million hectares of damaged and unused lands making suitable for cultivation, respectively (Li et al., 2014). There is still a long way ahead of 13th FYSP (2016 – 2020) expecting land consolidation program plan to achieve food security and to sustain social – economic and environmental developments of rural areas of China (Huang et al., 2011).

The private adaptation intention – behavior is widely stated in many behavioral and psychological studies. It has been recent, recognized and hot research topic in agricultural technology and climate change information adaptation studies (Subbiah et al., 2004; Hu et al., 2006; Harrison and Williams, 2007; Kumar, 2012; Arbuckle et al., 2015). Some literature investigates the private or collective adaptation intention is significantly affected by the availability and standards of information sources (Ziervogel et al. , 2005; Hu et al. , 2006; Artikov et al. , 2006; Harrison and Williams, 2007) . Burt (1987) also found Social – network and media play an important role in the development of private awareness and perception towards their surrounding as well as adaptation intentions decision – making. While other scholars argue that the private adaptation intention is not only influenced by the availability of information but also by the individual technical know – how, attitude, perception, and socioeconomic factors (Hassan and Nhemachena, 2008; Bryan et al. , 2009; Deressa et al. , 2009, 2011; Below et al. , 2012) .

The local farmers' awareness, perception and adaptation intention of sustainable land management technologies are not well documented in Sichuan province. Thus, examining the impact of land consolidation information sources (Social network and Media) in the development of individual or collective awareness, perception, and adaptation intention; and understanding the effect of private technical know – how, attitude and perception of land consolidation and rehabilitation program on the adaptation intention decisions is very important to the local government to authorize, update and promote the efforts of land consolidation and rehabilitation program in the province.

Therefore, the objectives of this chapter to: (a) to examine the farmers' awareness, perception, and adaptation intention towards land consolidation and rehabilitation program and; (b) to evaluate the contribution of Media and Social – network in the development of land consolidation awareness, perception and adaptation intention of rural Sichuan farmers. Additionally, this answering answering the following research questions: (i) to what extent Media influence the awareness, perception as well as land consolidation adaptation intentions of the farmers? (ii) to what extent the farmer's social relations (within the family, neighbor, the community and extension experts) influence their awareness, perception, and land consolidation adaptation intentions?; and finally, (iii) to what extent the awareness and perception of land consolidation and rehabilitation program implementing in their village influence the land consolidation adaptation intention the farmers?

4. 2   Conceptual framework and research assumptions

4. 2. 1   Conceptual framework

To address the motivation of smallholder farmers to adopt land consolidation program implemented in their village, we have developed a conceptual framework consists of three core components (Figure 1). The first core element is the land consolidation information sources which consist of two sub components such as Media and Social networks. The second core element is the land consolidation awareness and perception level which consists of two sub component land consolidation awareness and land consolidation perception themselves. The third and the final core component is the motivation of smallholder farmers to adopt land consolidation i. e adaptation intention.

4. 2. 2   Research hypothesis

Eight research hypotheses are formulated from our constructed conceptual framework and stated by unidirectional causality relationship among the latent variables. The hypotheses of this study are:

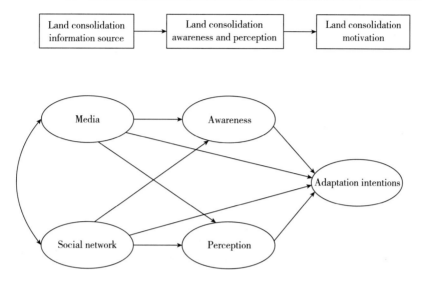

| Land consolidation information source | → | Land consolidation awareness and perception | → | Land consolidation motivation |

Figure 1 The conceptual framework of land consolidation adaptation

H1: Media has a positive and significant impact on the development of farmers' awareness towards land consolidation;

H2: Media has a positive and significant impact on the development of farmers' perception to land consolidation and rehabilitation programs implementing in their village;

H3: Media contribute a positive and significant role to perform farmers' land consolidation adaptation intention decisions;

H4: Social network has a positive and significant impact on the development of farmers' awareness towards land consolidation;

H5: Social network has a positive significant impact on the development of farmers' perception to land consolidation and rehabilitation programs implementing in their village;

H6: Social network contribute a positive and significant effect to perform farmers' land consolidation adaptation intention decisions;

H7: Farmers the more aware of land consolidation are the more intended to perform land consolidation adaptation decisions finally;

H8: Farmers the more perceived of land consolidation and rehabilitation program implementing in their village are the more intended to perform land consolidation adaptation decisions.

4. 3   Research methodology

4. 3. 1   Variable measurement

This study employed the SEM statistical technique to test the hypotheses and to synthesize the structural link between the construct variables of the conceptual framework. As showed in Figure 1, we have developed two exogenous latent variables and three endogenous latent variables to test hypotheses as well as to achieve the objectives of the study. Therefore, further variable setting scale design is required to make comprehensive measurement of latent variable by their observed variables.

Thus, a clear, simple and straightforward structured questionnaire was developed (see Appendix I) that can accurately measure the latent variables of the conceptual framework of the study. Based on theoretical models and research hypotheses, the latent variables that cannot be directly measured by the researcher are explained by the observable variables that can be measured. The specific measurement items of each observed variable are designed by means of five Likert scale that corresponding attribute scale design that comprehensively reflect latent variables. The reason we have choose the five Likert scale is smallholder farmers might not enable them to identify their level of agreement when the Likert scale is large (more than five). In addition many literature have been preferred five Likert scale rather seven. Therefore, this Chapter follows the mainstream research paradigm and adopts five level Likert scale as data collection tools. Therefore, the measurement items of all the observed variables involved in this paper adopt the Likert scale 5 (Table 1).

Table 1   Setting and measurement of research variables

Latent variables		Observed variables			Variable measurement
Variable name	Code	Variable name	Code	Descriptions	Likert Scale
Media	ξ1	Media 1	X1	I have accessed information on land consolidation and rehabilitation from Television and Radio.	1: Strongly disagree; 2: Disagree; 3: Uncertain; 4: Agree; 5: Strongly agree
		Media 2	X2	I have accessed information on land consolidation and rehabilitation from Newspapers.	
		Media 3	X3	I have read about land consolidation and rehabilitation from short communication materials (flyers, brochures, and posters).	
		Media 4	X4	I have explored information on land consolidation and rehabilitation from the Internet.	
Social network	ξ2	Social network 1	X5	I discusses about land consolidation and rehabilitation program with my family.	1: Strongly disagree; 2: Disagree; 3: Uncertain; 4: Agree; 5: Strongly agree
		Social network 2	X6	I discusses with my neighbors or farmers groups about land consolidation and rehabilitation program.	
		Social network 3	X7	I discusses with extension workers about land consolidation and rehabilitation program.	
		Social network 4	X8	I discuss with my community about land consolidation and rehabilitation program.	

continued Table

Latent variables		Observed variables			Variable measurement
Variable name	Code	Variable name	Code	Descriptions	Likert Scale
Awareness	η1	Awareness 1	Y1	Land consolidation is the practice of farm plot configuration in terms of size, shape, and layout.	1: Strongly disagree; 2: Disagree; 3: Uncertain; 4: Agree; 5: Strongly agree
		Awareness 2	Y2	Land consolidation improves the quality of land for production system including expanding irrigation and drainage systems, road networks which provide better access to plots for both labor and machinery.	
		Awareness 3	Y3	Land consolidation plays an important role in reducing land degradation as well as improving farmland productivity.	
		Awareness 4	Y4	Land consolidation reduce social conflict on irrigation water use and farm plot border by improving the irrigation water system and amount, and by providing clear farm plot demarcations among neighbor plots.	
		Awareness 5	Y5	I am happy and aware of land consolidation and rehabilitation program in my village.	
Perception	η2	Perception 1	Y6	Since the establishment of land consolidation and rehabilitation program in my village, the uneconomically dispersed small and irregular farmlands are changed to medium to high quality farmlands.	1: Strongly disagree; 2: Disagree; 3: Uncertain; 4: Agree; 5: Strongly agree
		Perception 2	Y7	Since the implementation of land consolidation and rehabilitation program in my village, the farm infrastructures such as irrigation and drainage systems, road networks are improving.	
		Perception 3	Y8	Since the implementation of land consolidation program in my village, our village becomes clean and tidy and more suitable for residence compares to before.	
		Perception 4	Y9	I believe the small, scattered and uneconomical fragmented farmlands will not be appear in my village in future.	
		Perception 5	Y10	The land consolidation and rehabilitation program in my village is the responsibility of me, my entire family, village, governmental and non-governmental officials, as well as researchers and academicians.	

continued Table

Latent variables		Observed variables			Variable measurement
Variable name	Code	Variable name	Code	Descriptions	Likert Scale
Adaptation intention	η3	Intention 1	Y11	I am always intend to use the recommended fertilizer on my land.	1: Strongly disagree; 2: Disagree; 3: Uncertain; 4: Agree; 5: Strongly agree
		Intention 2	Y12	I am always intend to use improved crop varieties.	
		Intention 3	Y13	I am always intend to rent in neighbor farmland from others.	
		Intention 4	Y14	I am always intend to have improve moderate and high quality farmlands.	
		Intention 5	Y15	I am always intend to use modern agricultural machinery.	
		Intention 6	Y16	I am always intend to have modern irrigation and drainage system in my farmland.	
		Intention 7	Y17	I am always intended to have a clean and clear village which is suitable for residence.	

The data of the scale mainly reflect the discrete choice data of respondents' subjective judgment. The attribute design of each observed variable in the scale is "strongly disagree", "disagree", "uncertain", "agree" and "strongly agree". The scale is designed to be 1 − 5, the minimum and maximum are respectively counted as 1 and 5, among them, 1 means "strongly disagree"; 2 means "disagree"; 3 means "uncertain"; 4 means "agree"; and 5 means "strongly agree".

4.3.1.1 Exogenous latent variables

Media (ξ1): Media is the collective communication outlet or tool that is used to store and deliver information or data. It provides information to users either in printing (Newspapers, flyers, brochures, leaflets) or electronic (radio and television) broadcasting or both. Media play an important role in environmental perception and awareness creation and inform the potential benefits and risks of environmental management to users. Korsching and Hoban (1990), Lichtenberg and Zimmerman (1999), and Toma and Mathijs (2007) found that Media play a positive impact on perception and awareness creation. Hence, this study evaluates to what extent electronic and printing Media influence the awareness, perception and adaptation intention of farmers towards land consolidation.

Social network ($\xi2$): It is a set of social structure deal with the social interactions of actors (individuals or organizations). According to social contagion theory, individuals collect and process information to form awareness and perception are influenced by her or his social network tie (Burt, 1987). Scherer and Cho (2003) argue that in risk perception and attitude analysis, the unit of analysis should not be an isolated individual, but rather the individual embedded in his or her social network. Thus, this study we examine the ability of individual farmer social interaction with others (within the family, neighbor, agricultural extension workers as well as the community) to gather and use land consolidation information. And, to what extent the social network affect the individual awareness, perception as well as adaptation intentions.

4.3.1.2 Endogenous latent variables

Awareness ($\eta1$): It is the attention, concern (mindful or heedful) and sensitivity of individuals to their surroundings (Sudarmadi et al. , 2001). In other words, an individual aware of the environmental problems are more conscious to understand the consequences of the environmental problems and, as a result, the person will more concerned about it. When an environmental phenomenon has been individually perceived, the awareness will further comprehend, interpreted, and evaluated regarding the decision making. In this research paper, we evaluate to what extent the awareness of land consolidation affects the adaptation intention decisions of the individual farmers.

Perception（η2）: It defined as the recognition of environmental phenomenon of individuals based on their memory and influenced prior of their experiences (Sudarmadi et al. , 2001). Individuals receive signals and stimuli from the social and physical environment around them and use to build – up understanding of the environment Phenomenon. The stimuli and signals are subjectively evaluated to form perception through a cognitive process of interacting with the environment. Thus, this paper we examine the farmers' perception towards land consolidation and rehabilitation program implementing in their village and to what extent it affect the adaptation intention mechanisms of the farmers.

Adaptation intention（η3）: Adaptation intention is the behavioral and psychological dynamics of the individual that adjust the variations in living conditions to improve their survival. Adaptation intention assesses what individuals want to achieve or intend in future. In another word, adaptation intention identifies the decision – making of individual farmers. It also helps to develop strategies to maximize benefit. Therefore, in this study, we expected that farmers to perform land consolidation adaptation intention decisions are to be influenced by Media and social network, as well as by the individual awareness and perception of land consolidation and rehabilitation program implementing in their village.

4. 3. 2   Estimation procedure

As we have discussed in Chapter three the SEM has two sub – models: the measurement model which specifies the relationship between the latent variables and their observed variables while the structural model represents the relationships between the latent exogenous and latent endogenous variables as well as the relationships among the latent endogenous variables.

The general framework of the measurement and structural models are mathematically expressed by equation $(4-1)$, equation $(4-2)$ and equation $(4-3)$ (Chapter IV) . The model estimation can be done by several software packages. Thus, in this study, the model fit criterion is estimated by Maximum Likelihood Estimate (MLE) as recommended by Joreskog and Sorbom (1996) and Hair et al. (2011) by means of IBM – AMOS 22. 0 version.

The conceptual model this study (Figure 2) and equation $(4-1)$, equation $(4-2)$ and equation $(4-3)$ which can be expressed in matrix form in the following mathematical model:

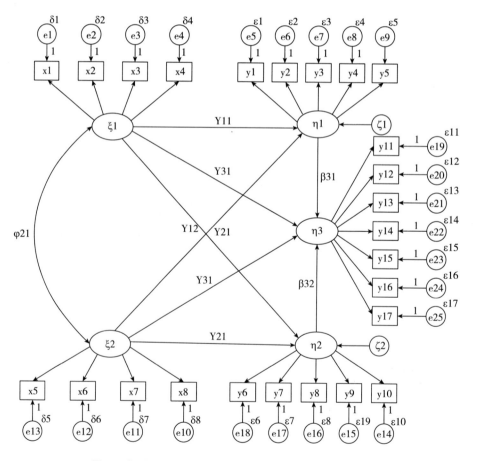

Figure 2　Land consolidation adaptation intention model

$$
\begin{bmatrix} x_1 \\ x_2 \\ x_3 \\ x_4 \\ x_5 \\ x_6 \\ x_7 \\ x_8 \end{bmatrix} = \begin{bmatrix} \lambda_{x1} & 0 \\ \lambda_{x2} & 0 \\ \lambda_{x3} & 0 \\ \lambda_{x4} & 0 \\ 0 & \lambda_{x5} \\ 0 & \lambda_{x6} \\ 0 & \lambda_{x7} \\ 0 & \lambda_{x8} \end{bmatrix} \begin{bmatrix} \xi_1 \\ \xi_2 \end{bmatrix} + \begin{bmatrix} \delta_1 \\ \delta_2 \\ \delta_3 \\ \delta_4 \\ \delta_5 \\ \delta_6 \\ \delta_7 \\ \delta_8 \end{bmatrix} \tag{4-1}
$$

$$
\begin{bmatrix} y_1 \\ y_2 \\ y_3 \\ y_4 \\ y_5 \\ y_6 \\ y_7 \\ y_8 \\ y_9 \\ y_{10} \\ y_{11} \\ y_{12} \\ y_{13} \\ y_{14} \\ y_{15} \\ y_{16} \\ y_{17} \end{bmatrix} = \begin{bmatrix} \lambda_{y1} & 0 & 0 \\ \lambda_{y2} & 0 & 0 \\ \lambda_{y3} & 0 & 0 \\ \lambda_{y4} & 0 & 0 \\ \lambda_{y5} & 0 & 0 \\ 0 & \lambda_{y6} & 0 \\ 0 & \lambda_{y7} & 0 \\ 0 & \lambda_{y8} & 0 \\ 0 & \lambda_{y9} & 0 \\ 0 & \lambda_{y10} & 0 \\ 0 & 0 & \lambda_{y11} \\ 0 & 0 & \lambda_{y12} \\ 0 & 0 & \lambda_{y13} \\ 0 & 0 & \lambda_{y14} \\ 0 & 0 & \lambda_{y15} \\ 0 & 0 & \lambda_{y16} \\ 0 & 0 & \lambda_{y17} \end{bmatrix} \begin{bmatrix} \eta_1 \\ \eta_2 \\ \eta_3 \end{bmatrix} + \begin{bmatrix} \varepsilon_1 \\ \varepsilon_2 \\ \varepsilon_3 \\ \varepsilon_4 \\ \varepsilon_5 \\ \varepsilon_6 \\ \varepsilon_7 \\ \varepsilon_8 \\ \varepsilon_9 \\ \varepsilon_{10} \\ \varepsilon_{11} \\ \varepsilon_{12} \\ \varepsilon_{13} \\ \varepsilon_{14} \\ \varepsilon_{15} \\ \varepsilon_{16} \\ \varepsilon_{17} \end{bmatrix} \tag{4-2}
$$

$$
\begin{bmatrix} \eta_1 \\ \eta_2 \\ \eta_3 \end{bmatrix} = \begin{bmatrix} 0 & 0 & 0 \\ 0 & 0 & 0 \\ \beta_{3,1} & \beta_{3,2} & 0 \end{bmatrix} \begin{bmatrix} \eta_1 \\ \eta_2 \\ \eta_3 \end{bmatrix} + \begin{bmatrix} \gamma_{1,1} \gamma_{1,2} \\ \gamma_{2,1} \gamma_{2,2} \\ \gamma_{3,1} \gamma_{3,2} \end{bmatrix} \begin{bmatrix} \xi_1 \\ \xi_2 \end{bmatrix} + \begin{bmatrix} \zeta_1 \\ \zeta_2 \\ \zeta_3 \end{bmatrix} \qquad (4-3)
$$

4. 4　Results

4. 4. 1　Descriptive statistics of the respondent

The individual characteristics of stallholder farmer's unit sample is presented in Table 2. The result showed that the male headed household are 57% whereas the female headed households are 43%. The higher age distribution of the respondents of age range is from 41 to 60 years old (61. 3%), followed by 61 – 80 years old (26. 6%) and the remaining 12. 1% are 21 to 40 years old. The majority of the respondents are able to read and write and attended primary and above school (98. 8%) whereas the remaining 1. 2% are illiterate. This might indicate that the sample farmers have some knowledge about modern farming system and land consolidation program implemented in their village. Further, more than 83% of the respondents have 20 and higher farming experience. 94% of the respondent are agriculture is their primary source of livelihood while less than 6% are mainly occupied primarily on non – agricultural livelihood such as trade, masonry and so on. More than half of the respondents (51%) have 0. 26 to 0. 50 ha farmland size and 32% are between 0. 01 to 0. 25 ha while the remaining 17% is 0. 50 ha and above farmland size. 39% of the respondents have 50000 RMB and less annual income and 30% of the respondent have annual income from 50000 to 210000

RMB, whereas the remaining 1% have no income.

Table 2 Demographic descriptive statistics of the respondent

Variables		Frequency	Percent	S. D
Sex	Male	189	57.1	0.49
	Female	142	42.9	
Age	21 – 40	40	12.1	0.61
	41 – 60	203	61.3	
	61 – 80	88	26.6	
Education	Illiterate	4	1.2	0.69
	Primary (1 – 6 grade)	180	54.4	
	Secondary (7 – 10 grade)	116	35.0	
	High School (11 – 12 grade)	30	9.1	
	Collage	1	0.3	
Farming experience	3 – 20	57	17.2	0.63
	21 – 40	199	60.1	
	41 – 60	75	22.7	
Main occupation	Agriculture	312	94.3	0.23
	Non – agriculture	19	5.7	
Farm size (ha)	0.01 – 0.25	105	31.7	0.74
	0.26 – 0.50	170	51.4	
	0.50 – 1.00	47	14.2	
	1.01 – 1.80	9	2.7	
Annual income (CNY)	No income	4	1.2	0.92
	1000 – 20000	126	38.1	
	21000 – 50000	103	31.1	
	51000 – 100000	84	25.4	
	101000 – 210000	14	4.2	

Note: S. D is the standard deviation. Number respondent (N = 331)

In summary, the descriptive statistical analysis result more importantly used to en-sure the reliability and validity of the questionnaire scale and the individual sample has a good representation, through the individual characteristics of a comprehensive reflection

of the sample. Therefore, the sample farm household data can be used for empirical a-
nalysis of structural equation model to test the hypothesis of land consolidation adaptation
intentions proposed in this chapter to verify the theoretical model.

4. 4. 2　Descriptive statistics of the variables

Using SPSS 22. 0 statistical software the 331 sample individual statistical data 25
observation variables questionnaire data set of the land consolidation adaptation intention
of Sichuan smallholder farmers is presented in Table 3. The statistical results show that
the mean level of agreement regard to the Media's observed variables are range from
3. 13 to 3. 66 with overall mean score of latent variable (Media) 3. 43. The average
score of social network observed variables are ranged from 3. 82 to 3. 95 with overall
mean of latent variable is 3. 90 (Social network). The awareness's observed variables
mean level of agreement ranges from 3. 75 to 3. 99 score with an overall latent variable
mean of 3. 93 (Awareness). Whereas the overall perception latent variable mean score
showed that 3. 67 with observed variable mean score range from 3. 56 to 3. 88. Further,
the overall average level of agreement for adaptation intention latent variable is 4. 08
with mean observed variables range from 4. 03 to 4. 21 score level. The result indicated
media has the lower score level and followed by perception compare to social network,
awareness and adaptation intention latent variables, respectively. From the standard deviation perspectives, the standard deviations of all observed variables are in the range of
0. 54 to 0. 95 which is less than 1 that the largest standard deviation was found in perception latent variable whereas the smallest standard deviation found in awareness latent
variable. The higher level of agreement for all observed variables and latent variables
were 5 whereas the minimum level of agreement is for media and adaptation intention 1,
and for awareness, perception and social network is 2. The higher mode value is 4 and

the lower mode value is 3. In addition the higher median score level of the observed vari-

ables were 4 while the minimum is 3. The overall descriptive statistics result showed

that, the data has a good representation, indicating that the variables set in this re-

search are more reasonable. Thus, all the research variables selected in this paper can

be used for the structural equation measurement model to meet the needs of building the

conceptual model and empirical model of the structural equation of land consolidation

adaptation intention.

Table 3   Descriptive statistics of the variables

Latent variables		Observed variables			Max	Min	Mode	Median	Mean	S. D
Variable name	Code	Variable name	Code	No. items						
Media (MDI)	ξ1	Media 1	X1	4	5	1	4	4	3. 66	0. 90
		Media 2	X2		5	1	3	3	3. 32	0. 73
		Media 3	X3		5	1	4	4	3. 60	0. 80
		Media 4	X4		5	1	3	3	3. 13	0. 88
Social network (NTW)	ξ2	Social network 1	X5	4	5	2	4	4	3. 82	0. 68
		Social network 2	X6		5	2	4	4	3. 92	0. 66
		Social network 3	X7		5	2	4	4	3. 91	0. 67
		Social network 4	X8		5	2	4	4	3. 95	0. 62
Awareness (AWR)	η1	Awareness 1	Y1		5	2	4	4	3. 93	0. 54
		Awareness 2	Y2		5	3	4	4	3. 98	0. 56
		Awareness 3	Y3		5	2	4	4	3. 75	0. 68
		Awareness 4	Y4		5	2	4	4	3. 99	0. 58
		Awareness 5	Y5		5	2	4	4	3. 99	0. 58
Perception (PRC)	η2	Perception 1	Y6	5	5	2	4	4	3. 60	0. 87
		Perception 2	Y7		5	2	4	4	3. 72	0. 86
		Perception 3	Y8		5	2	4	4	3. 88	0. 83
		Perception 4	Y9		5	2	4	4	3. 56	0. 87
		Perception 5	Y10		5	2	4	4	3. 60	0. 95

Latent variables		Observed variables			Max	Min	Mode	Median	Mean	S. D
Variable name	Code	Variable name	Code	No. items						
Adaptation intention（INT）	η3	Intention 1	Y11	7	5	1	4	4	4. 09	0. 69
		Intention 2	Y12		5	2	4	4	4. 17	0. 62
		Intention 3	Y13		5	2	4	4	4. 03	0. 78
		Intention 4	Y14		5	2	4	4	4. 21	0. 62
		Intention 5	Y15		5	1	4	4	4. 17	0. 69
		Intention 6	Y16		5	1	4	4	4. 24	0. 63
		Intention 7	Y17		5	2	4	4	3. 66	0. 90

4. 4. 3　Data adequacy, consistency and validity checking

Prior to SEM model estimation, it is required to test the sampling adequacy, internal consistency and validity of the sample survey data (Teguh Sambodo, 2007). Reliability and validity are two important indexes to measure the questionnaire data quality of reliability and validity. These two indexes can evaluate the model stability of measurement tools and the validity of measurement items in order to ensure that the collected credible and effective data to satisfy the objective and validity of the constructed theoretical model of structure equation model verification and ensure the internal validity of the research conclusion. Since the data in this article comes from the field survey, the sample data reliability and validity test was estimated by Cronbach's alpha coefficient and KMO using SPSS statistical software for factor analysis develop model.

4. 4. 3. 1　Data reliability test

The reliability of the scale refers to the consistency, stability and reliability of the results obtained from the measurement tools and is an indication of the true extent of the measured features. The Cronbach's alpha coefficient is the most commonly used reliability indicator for the internal consistency of social science research. The Cronbach's alpha value lies between 0 and 1, and the value closer to 1, the higher the reliability and internal consistency. In general, a Cronbach's alpha coefficient greater than 0.60 means that the scale of reliability is acceptable, 0.70 – 0.80 means the scale has a high degree of confidence, while a scale greater than 0.90 means the scale reliability is very high.

The reliability and internal consistency test of 331 valid sample data of Sichuan smallholder result is presented in Table 4. The result showed that, the Cronbach's alpha coefficient of the five latent constructs as well as the entire model variables were higher than the minimum Cronbach's alpha cut – off value (0.70) (Hair et al., 2010). The minimum Cronbach's alpha coefficient was found in Media latent variable with 0.709 value. Equal Cronbach's alpha value was found in awareness and perception latent variable with 0.856 value. Whereas, greater scale of Cronbach alpha was found 0.13 and 0.914 value for Social network and adaptation intention latent constructs, respectively. Further, the Cronbach alpha coefficient of the entire latent variables were 0.907 value. The test results show that: (a) the internal consistency of each sub – scale and the total is great, and the reliability of each scale is higher; (b) there is a strong correlation between the corresponding observed variables of each latent variable, the internal structure of each latent variable has a good consistency, and each scale has good stability and reliability. Therefore, the overall reliability of the survey questionnaire of land consolidation adaptation intention designed is relatively high. Additionally, as showed in Table 4, the determinant values of the latent constructs as well as the entire variables are positive which indicate that there is no multicollinearity and a computational problem for factor analysis (Field, 2009).

Table 4 Reliability test scale and internal consistency result

Latent variables		Observed variables		No. items	Cronbach's Alpha (α)	Determinant value
Variable name	Code	Variable name	Code			
Media (MDI)	ξ1	Media 1	X1	4	0. 709	0. 285
		Media 2	X2			
		Media 3	X3			
		Media 4	X4			
Social network (NTW)	ξ2	Social network 1	X5	4	0. 913	0. 063
		Social network 2	X6			
		Social network 3	X7			
		Social network 4	X8			
Awareness (AWR)	η1	Awareness 1	Y1	5	0. 856	0. 116
		Awareness 2	Y2			
		Awareness 3	Y3			
		Awareness 4	Y4			
		Awareness 5	Y5			
Perception (PRC)	η2	Perception 1	Y6	5	0. 856	0. 102
		Perception 2	Y7			
		Perception 3	Y8			
		Perception 4	Y9			
		Perception 5	Y10			
Adaptation intention (INT)	η3	Intention 1	Y11	7	0. 914	0. 010
		Intention 2	Y12			
		Intention 3	Y13			
		Intention 4	Y14			
		Intention 5	Y15			
		Intention 6	Y16			
		Intention 7	Y17			
The entire variables				25	0. 907	3. 283E − 7

4. 4. 3. 2 Validity test result

Validity refers, how much the measurement index or measurement item can explain a certain structural feature accurately and effectively (Wu Minglong, 2013). The validity of constructiveness mainly verifies the validity of the aggregate and the discriminant validity between the latent variables and a group of observed variables to which they belong, and usually uses the factor loading value. Kaiser – Meyer – Olkin (KMO) and Bartlett test of Sphericity measures the sampling adequacy and suitability of the survey data for factor analysis and model development.

KMO coefficient is usually considered more than 0.50 for factor analysis and KMO value less than 0.50 is not suitable for factor analysis. The KMO value greater than 0.70 means that factor analysis is better, indicating that there is a certain correlation between the variables, the sample data is more suitable for factor analysis. As showed in Table 5, the KMO values for all latent variables are above the minimum cut – off value of 0.5 (Kaiser, 1974) and ranges between 0.719 and 0.899 and the Bartlett's test of Sphericity of each latent variables is also significant at 0.0001 significant level. In addition, the entire variable KMO values is 0.894 which is above the required standard KMO value (0.50), the Bartlett's test of sample distribution had an approximate chi – square value of 4789.79, a degree of freedom of 300 and highly significant at P – value < 0.001. The result reveals that there is sufficient sampling adequacy available and suitable for factor analysis and the effect is ideal.

Table 5 Data adequacy and suitability result

Latent variables		Observed variables			KMO	Bartlett's Test		
Variable name	Code	Variable name	Code	No. items		Chi – square	df	Sig.
Media (MDI)	ξ1	Media 1	X1	4	0.719	295.17	6	***
		Media 2	X2					
		Media 3	X3					
		Media 4	X4					

Continued Table

Latent variables		Observed variables			KMO	Bartlett's Test		
Variable name	Code	Variable name	Code	No. items		Chi – square	df	Sig.
Social network (NTW)	ξ2	Social network 1	X5	4	0.844	906.28	6	***
		Social network 2	X6					
		Social network 3	X7					
		Social network 4	X8					
Awareness (AWR)	η1	Awareness 1	Y1	5	0.825	704.86	10	***
		Awareness 2	Y2					
		Awareness 3	Y3					
		Awareness 4	Y4					
		Awareness 5	Y5					
Perception (PRC)	η2	Perception 1	Y6	5	0.810	747.24	10	***
		Perception 2	Y7					
		Perception 3	Y8					
		Perception 4	Y9					
		Perception 5	Y10					
Adaptation intention (INT)	η3	Intention 1	Y11	7	0.899	1504.36	21	***
		Intention 2	Y12					
		Intention 3	Y13					
		Intention 4	Y14					
		Intention 5	Y15					
		Intention 6	Y16					
		Intention 7	Y17					
The entire variables				25	0.894	4789.79	300	***

4.4.3.3 Factor loading (λ), Average Variance Estimate (AVE) and Composite Reliability

Factor loading (λ) tests that to what extent the observed variables are strongly related to associate latent constructs in factor analysis. The minimum standardized cut – off value of factor loading for latent construct and observed variables is 0.7 and 0.5, respectively and should be statistically significant (Hair et al. , 2010) . As showed in Table 6, the average standardized factor loadings coefficient for adaptation intention, perception, social network, awareness, and media is 0. 783, 0. 732, 0. 835, 0. 724, and 0. 638, respectively. In addition, the standardized factor loadings coefficient of the observed variables are above the minimum threshold factor loading value of (0. 5) except for Media 4 (X4) and are statistically significant. Hence, the overall factor loading result validates that the conceptual framework latent constructs are strongly explained by their observed variables.

Further, the Composite Reliability (CR) and Average Variance Extracted (AVE) of the five latent constructs were calculated using equation 9 and 10 respectively. The CR indicates the degree to which the observed variables explain the latent construct whereas the AVE measures the amount of variance captured by construct through its items (observed variables) in comparison to the amount of variance captured due to the measurement error (Fornell and Larcker, 1981; Bagozzi and Yi, 1988; Hair et al. , 2010) . According to Gefen et al. (2000) and Hair et al. (2010), the minimum cut – off value for CR and AVE is 0. 7 and 0. 5 respectively. As shown in Table 6, the CR value of all the latent constructs of this study range between 0. 734 and 0. 918. The result verified that the construct latent variables are explained by the observed variables and support to precede factor analysis. Additionally, the AVE values of the latent constructs are above the standard threshold except for media (ξ1) (0. 429) . The result reveals that there is no convergence concern between the latent constructs and observed variables to develop the model except for Media.

Despite the AVE value of latent variable media is less than the minimum cut – off (0. 429), Hair et al. (2010) confirm that there is no convergence concern if the AVE value of any two latent constructs is higher than their square correlation estimates the variables are truly distinct each other (Table 7).

Table 6 Factor loading (λ), Average Variance Estimate

(AVE) and Composite Reliability (CR)

Latent variables		Observed variables			Factor loading (λ)	AVE	CR
Variable name	Code	Variable name	Code	No. items			
Media (MDI)	ξ1	Media 1	X1	4	0.715***	0.429	0.734
		Media 2	X2		0.636***		
		Media 3	X3		0.812ᵃ		
		Media 4	X4		0.384***		
Social network (NTW)	ξ2	Social network 1	X5	4	0.830***	0.726	0.914
		Social network 2	X6		0.861***		
		Social network 3	X7		0.853ᵃ		
		Social network 4	X8		0.798***		
Awareness (AWR)	η1	Awareness 1	Y1	5	0.755***	0.548	0.858
		Awareness 2	Y2		0.746***		
		Awareness 3	Y3		0.850ᵃ		
		Awareness 4	Y4		0.679***		
		Awareness 5	Y5		0.590***		
Perception (PRC)	η2	Perception 1	Y6	5	0.637***	0.547	0.857
		Perception 2	Y7		0.708***		
		Perception 3	Y8		0.792ᵃ		
		Perception 4	Y9		0.795***		
		Perception 5	Y10		0.730***		
Adaptation intention (INT)	η3	Intention 1	Y11	7	0.701***	0.616	0.918
		Intention 2	Y12		0.829***		
		Intention 3	Y13		0.764ᵃ		
		Intention 4	Y14		0.885***		
		Intention 5	Y15		0.764***		
		Intention 6	Y16		0.816***		
		Intention 7	Y17		0.721***		

Note: *** significant at 1%. "a" are values that are not calculated due to the loading set to 1.0 to control construct variance.

Table 7 Discriminant validity test results

Construct		Media	Social network	Awareness	Perception	Adaptation intention
		ξ1	ξ2	η1	η2	η3
Media	ξ1	0. 655				
Social network	ξ2	0. 294 (0. 086) ***	0. 740			
Awareness	η1	0. 325 (0. 106) ***	0. 389 (0. 151) ***	0. 852		
Perception	η2	0. 314 (0. 098) ***	0. 434 (0. 188) ***	0. 606 (0. 367) ***	0. 785	
Adaptation intention	η3	0. 370 (0. 137) ***	0. 512 (0. 262) ***	0. 453 (0. 205) ***	0. 499 (0. 249) ***	0. 740
Mean		3. 424	3. 90	3. 93	3. 67	4. 17
S. D.		0. 826	0. 657	0. 586	0. 875	0. 656

Note: *** is significant at 0. 001 level. The diagonal elements shown in bold indicate the SQR – AVE and the other is the correlation matrix with the square of correlation in parentheses.

4. 4. 3. 4 Discriminant and convergent validity

The discriminant and convergent validity is presented in Table 7 and Table 8, respectively. As showed in Table 7, the correlation matrix among latent construct variables is positive and significant. The discriminant validity concern between two latent constructs can assess by comparing the square root of AVE (SQR – AVE) value and their correlation coefficients. Fornell and Larcker (1981) suggest that if the SQR – AVE value is greater than the correlation coefficient, thus, there is no discriminant concern to precede factor analysis and develop the model. The result showed that, the SQR – AVE value of each construct variable is greater than the correlation coefficient between them. The result validated that, there is a high degree of discrimination between the latent variables.

Further, as stated in Table 8, the standardized path coefficient of the measurement model latent variables to their corresponding observed variables are in the range of 0. 329 to 0. 875 and significant at 0. 0001 level. In addition, the critical ratios (C. R.) value of all the observed variables are in the range of 5. 376 to 19. 967 which are greater than the minimum standard (C. R. > 3. 28) . The results revealed that, all the observed variables converge to their corresponding latent variables, and all the latent variables have good explanatory power for their observed indicators. In general explanation, the five latent variables have higher convergence validity.

Table 8   Convergent validity of measurement model

Path relationship	Unstandardized estimate	S. E.	C. R.	P – value	Standardized estimate
X1←ξ1	0. 941	0. 087	10. 842	∗∗∗	0. 703
X2←ξ1	0. 696	0. 068	10. 241	∗∗∗	0. 645
X3←ξ1	1. 000	—	—	—	0. 835
X4←ξ1	0. 429	0. 080	5. 376	∗∗∗	0. 329
X5←ξ2	1. 038	0. 055	19. 037	∗∗∗	0. 849
X6←ξ2	1. 000	—	—	—	0. 846
X7←ξ2	1. 061	0. 053	19. 967	∗∗∗	0. 875
X8←ξ2	0. 937	0. 050	18. 646	∗∗∗	0. 838
Y1←η1	0. 822	0. 070	11. 681	∗∗∗	0. 720
Y2←η1	0. 946	0. 074	12. 796	∗∗∗	0. 802
Y3←η1	1. 000	—	—	—	0. 694
Y4←η1	0. 917	0. 076	12. 034	∗∗∗	0. 745
Y5←η1	0. 902	0. 076	11. 902	∗∗∗	0. 735
Y6←η2	0. 988	0. 081	12. 147	∗∗∗	0. 716
Y7←η2	1. 028	0. 080	12. 846	∗∗∗	0. 759
Y8←η2	1. 069	0. 078	13. 719	∗∗∗	0. 818
Y9←η2	1. 000	—	—	—	0. 728
Y10←η2	1. 000	0. 088	11. 363	∗∗∗	0. 669
Y11←η3	0. 995	0. 064	15. 461	∗∗∗	0. 745
Y12←η3	0. 969	0. 056	17. 367	∗∗∗	0. 808
Y13←η3	1. 055	0. 074	14. 183	∗∗∗	0. 700

Continued Table

Path relationship	Unstandardized estimate	S. E.	C. R.	P – value	Standardized estimate
Y14←η3	1. 000	—	—	—	0. 831
Y15←η3	1. 030	0. 063	16. 31	***	0. 774
Y16←η3	1. 028	0. 055	18. 721	***	0. 849
Y17←η3	0. 853	0. 052	16. 475	***	0. 779

Note: *** is significant at P < 0. 0001, S. E is standard error, C. R. is Critical Ratio.

In summary, the pre – SEM model estimation survey data checking results such as Cronbach's alpha, KMO, determinant value, factor loading, CR, AVE, Correlation matrix and SQR – AVE of the observed items and their associate latent constructs are at an acceptable range and support to precede factor analysis and develop the model. Therefore, the next step is determining the structural model Goodness – of – Fit (GoF) indexes for factor analysis using Maximum Likelihood Estimate (MLE).

4. 4. 4   Confirmatory Factor Analysis (CFA)

4. 4. 4. 1   Goodness of fit model checking

Once the collected data adequacy and consistency measures of the construct variables are at an acceptable range and allow to build a model. The next step is the structural model goodness of fit checking is done using AMOS 22. 0 statistical software package for Maximum Likelihood Estimate (MLE). Therefore, the overall fitness test of the structural model for land consolidation adaptation intention classified into Chi – square indexes, absolute fit indexes, incremental fit indexes and parsimony fit indexes as suggested by hair et al. (2010). The overall structural model goodness of fit result is presented in Table 9.

The result indicate that the Chi – square (χ^2) is 632. 851, the degree of freedom

(df) is 265 and significant at p < 0.0001 level. The normed Chi – square (χ^2/df) value is 2.354 and according to Kline (1998) and Hair et al. (2011) suggestion the normed Chi – square value less than 3.0 is acceptable. The absolute fit indexes such as Goodness – of – fit Index (GFI) and Adjusted Goodness – of – Fit Index (AGFI) is 0.870 and 0.841, 0.854, respectively which are less than the standard cut – off value of 0.90 (Hair et al., 2010). However, Byrne (2001), Kline (1998), Chau and Hu (2001) and Do Valle et al. (2005) suggest that the GFI and AGFI value greater than 0.80 can be considered as moderately acceptable. The Root Mean Square Error of Approximation (RMSEA), Root Mean Square Residual (RMR) and Standardized Root Mean Residual (SRMR) values are at the required standard values. RMSEA is 0.064 which is less than 0.08 standard value and ideal (Hair et al., 2010). The RMR and SRMR value is 0.026 and 0.049, which is also less than the cut – off value of 0.05 and 0.10, respectively (Hair et al., 2010). The result implies that the standardized and unstandardized difference between the observed correlation and predicted correlation is excellent. The incremental indexes such as Tucker – Lewis Fit Index (TLI), Incremental Fit index (IFI) and Comparative Fit Index (CFI) values are above the minimum standards value of 0.90 whereas, the Normed Fit Index is 0.873 that is lower than the required standards. According to Tucker and Lewis (1973), the TLI measures the model's fit improvement of the observed co – variance structure over a null model and typically range between 0 and 1. Thus, the TLI result of the measurement model indicates that 0.912 which is above the minimum acceptable threshold level of (TLI > 0.90) (Hair et al., 2010). This implies that there is a sufficient degree of correlation between the construct variables and their observed variables. The Comparative Fit Index (CFI) has been considered as a type of stable fit indexes which exhibits a fair degree of robustness (Anderson and Gerbing, 1992). A model having the CFI value above minimum acceptable limits (CFI > 0. 90) describe that there is a good degree of fit between the research framework and the data (Hair et al. , 2010) . The CFI value of the structural model indicates that 0. 923 and which above the minimum acceptable threshold. Thus, the CFI result reveals that the research framework and the survey data are adequately fit. Additionally, the Parsimony fit indexes are above the minimum standards. Thus, according to the model fit criterion, the overall structural model goodness – of – fit result indicates at acceptable ranges. Therefore, the proposed smallholder farmers land consolidation adaptation intention conceptual framework of this study has no required modification to improve the structural model because any model modification is strongly supported by the literature (Hair et al. , 2010) .

Table 9   Structural model goodness of fit result

Model fit indexes criteria			Statistics result	Statistics standards	Remark
Chi – square indexes	Chi – square	CMIN (χ^2)	623. 851	P < 0. 05	Good
	Normed Chi – square	CMIN/df	2. 354	< 3. 0	Good
Absolute fit indexes	Goodness of Fit Index	GFI	0. 870	> 0. 90	Ideal
	Adjusted Goodness of Fit Index	AGFI	0. 841	> 0. 90	Ideal
	Root Mean Square Error Approximation	RMSEA	0. 064	< 0. 08	Excellent
	Root Mean Square Residual	RMR	0. 026	< 0. 05	Excellent
	Standardized Root Mean Square Residual	SRMR	0. 049	< 0. 10	Excellent
Incremental indexes	Normed Fit Index	NFI	0. 873	> 0. 90	Ideal
	Incremental Fit Index	IFI	0. 923	> 0. 90	Good
	Tucker Lewis Index	TLI	0. 912	> 0. 90	Good
	Comparative Fit Index	CFI	0. 922	> 0. 90	Good
Parsimony fit indexes	Parsimony Normed Fit Index	PNFI	0. 771	> 0. 50	Good
	Parsimony Goodness of Fit Index	PGFI	0. 709	> 0. 50	Good
	Parsimony Comparative Fit Index	PCFI	0. 815	> 0. 50	Good

4. 4. 4. 2   Structural model parameters estimation result

IBM – AMOS is a powerful statistical software that provide the direction, size and significance of research parameters for evaluating the strength of the correlation between variables as well as the causal relationship among them in tabular and path diagrams. Based on the proposed conceptual framework of this study (Section 4. 2. 1), the empirical result of the structural equation model is presented in Figure 3 and the final model parameter significance test results is existed in Table 10. The estimated parameters of the structural model of land consolidation adaptation intention are standardized and estimated by means of IBM – AMOS 22. 0 statistical software for Maximum Likelihood Estimate (MLE). The result indicates that the standardized and unstandardized estimation coefficient of the structural model result are statistically significant except media ($\xi1$) to adaptation intention ($\eta3$). In addition, the measurement model showed that all the latent constructs are significantly explained by their observed variables at $p < 0.001$ significant level. The variance among latent exogenous variables ($\xi1$ and $\xi2$) and the measurement error matrix of the two endogenous latent variables ($\zeta1 \leftrightarrow \zeta2$) are highly significant.

Table 10   Parameter estimation result of structural equation in the level of Smallholder farmers land consolidation adaptation intentions, Sichuan Province, China

Parameter	Unstandardized Estimate	Standardized Estimate		S. E.	C. R.	P
		Structural Model				
$\eta1 \leftarrow \xi1$	0. 174 ***	0. 249 ***	(H1)	0. 047	3. 742	0. 000
$\eta1 \leftarrow \xi2$	0. 297 ***	0. 372 ***	(H4)	0. 051	5. 779	0. 000
$\eta2 \leftarrow \xi2$	0. 377 ***	0. 328 ***	(H5)	0. 073	5. 162	0. 000
$\eta2 \leftarrow \xi1$	0. 188 **	0. 187 **	(H2)	0. 067	2. 801	0. 005
$\eta3 \leftarrow \eta2$	0. 113 *	0. 140 *	(H8)	0. 049	2. 287	0. 022

Continued Table

Parameter	Unstandardized Estimate	Standardized Estimate		S. E.	C. R.	P
$\eta3 \leftarrow \eta1$	0. 242 **	0. 209 **	(H7)	0. 077	3. 133	0. 002
$\eta3 \leftarrow \xi2$	0. 408 ***	0. 440 ***	(H6)	0. 058	7. 012	0. 000
$\eta3 \leftarrow \xi1$	0. 043 ^{ns}	0. 053 ^{ns}	(H3)	0. 046	0. 932	0. 351
Measurement Model						
$X1 \leftarrow \xi1$	0. 941 ***	0. 703 ***		0. 087	10. 842	0. 000
$X2 \leftarrow \xi1$	0. 696 ***	0. 645 ***		0. 068	10. 241	0. 000
$X3 \leftarrow \xi1$	1. 000	0. 835		—	—	—
$X4 \leftarrow \xi1$	0. 429 ***	0. 329 ***		0. 080	5. 376	0. 000
$X5 \leftarrow \xi2$	0. 978 ***	0. 849 ***		0. 049	20. 091	0. 000
$X6 \leftarrow \xi2$	0. 942 ***	0. 846 ***		0. 047	19. 967	0. 000
$X7 \leftarrow \xi2$	1. 000 ***	0. 875 ***		—	—	—
$X8 \leftarrow \xi2$	0. 883 ***	0. 838 ***		0. 045	19. 637	0. 000
$Y1 \leftarrow \eta1$	0. 822 ***	0. 720 ***		0. 070	11. 681	0. 000
$Y2 \leftarrow \eta1$	0. 946 ***	0. 802 ***		0. 074	12. 796	0. 000
$Y3 \leftarrow \eta1$	1. 000	0. 694		—	—	—
$Y4 \leftarrow \eta1$	0. 917 ***	0. 745 ***		0. 076	12. 034	0. 000
$Y5 \leftarrow \eta1$	0. 902 ***	0. 735 ***		0. 076	11. 902	0. 000
$Y6 \leftarrow \eta2$	0. 924 ***	0. 716 ***		0. 069	13. 470	0. 000
$Y7 \leftarrow \eta2$	0. 962 ***	0. 759 ***		0. 067	14. 427	0. 000
$Y8 \leftarrow \eta2$	1. 000	0. 818		—	—	—
$Y9 \leftarrow \eta2$	0. 935 ***	0. 728 ***		0. 068	13. 719	0. 000
$Y10 \leftarrow \eta2$	0. 936 ***	0. 669 ***		0. 075	12. 429	0. 000
$Y11 \leftarrow \eta3$	0. 943 ***	0. 745 ***		0. 074	12. 787	0. 000
$Y12 \leftarrow \eta3$	0. 919 ***	0. 808 ***		0. 067	13. 806	0. 000
$Y13 \leftarrow \eta3$	1. 000	0. 700		—	—	—
$Y14 \leftarrow \eta3$	0. 948 ***	0. 831 ***		0. 067	14. 183	0. 000
$Y15 \leftarrow \eta3$	0. 977 ***	0. 774 ***		0. 074	13. 255	0. 000
$Y16 \leftarrow \eta3$	0. 975 ***	0. 849 ***		0. 067	14. 459	0. 000
$Y17 \leftarrow \eta3$	0. 808 ***	0. 779 ***		0. 061	13. 344	0. 000
Covariance						
$\xi1 \leftrightarrow \xi2$	0. 128 ***	0. 325 ***		0. 027	4. 767	0. 000
$\zeta1 \leftrightarrow \zeta2$	0. 093 ***	0. 379 ***		0. 019	4. 972	0. 000

Note: ***, **, *, respectively, by 0. 001, 0. 01, 0. 05 statistical significance level test. ^{ns} is not significant. H1 − 8 are the hypothesis of the study.

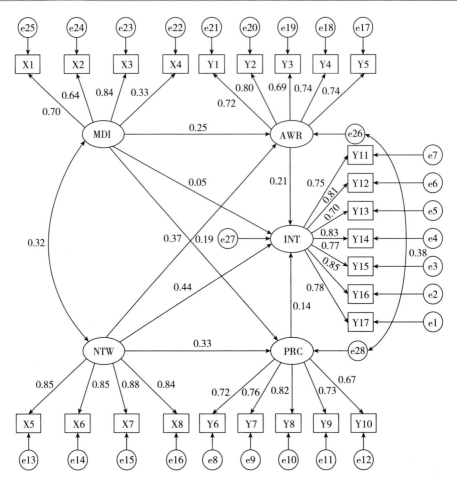

Figure 3   The standardized estimate result of the level of Smallholder farmers land consolidation adaptation intentions, Sichuan province, China

Media and Social – network significantly predict the land consolidation perception and awareness of the farmers that implemented in their village. Additionally, social – network, awareness, and perception significantly predict the smallholder farmers land consolidation adaptation intention decisions. However, the Media did not predict significantly the farmers' adaptation intention towards land consolidation.

The estimation results can be expressed in matrix form in the following mathematical model:

$$
\begin{bmatrix} x_1 \\ x_2 \\ x_3 \\ x_4 \\ x_5 \\ x_6 \\ x_7 \\ x_8 \end{bmatrix} = \begin{bmatrix} 0.703 & 0 \\ 0.645 & 0 \\ 0.835 & 0 \\ 0.329 & 0 \\ 0 & 0.849 \\ 0 & 0.846 \\ 0 & 0.875 \\ 0 & 0.838 \end{bmatrix} \begin{bmatrix} \xi_1 \\ \xi_2 \end{bmatrix} + \begin{bmatrix} 0.495 \\ 0.416 \\ 0.697 \\ 0.108 \\ 0.721 \\ 0.715 \\ 0.766 \\ 0.702 \end{bmatrix} \tag{4-4}
$$

$$
\begin{bmatrix} y_1 \\ y_2 \\ y_3 \\ y_4 \\ y_5 \\ y_6 \\ y_7 \\ y_8 \\ y_9 \\ y_{10} \\ y_{11} \\ y_{12} \\ y_{13} \\ y_{14} \\ y_{15} \\ y_{16} \\ y_{17} \end{bmatrix} = \begin{bmatrix} 0.720 & 0 & 0 \\ 0.802 & 0 & 0 \\ 0.694 & 0 & 0 \\ 0.745 & 0 & 0 \\ 0.735 & 0 & 0 \\ 0 & 0.716 & 0 \\ 0 & 0.759 & 0 \\ 0 & 0.818 & 0 \\ 0 & 0.728 & 0 \\ 0 & 0.669 & 0 \\ 0 & 0 & 0.745 \\ 0 & 0 & 0.808 \\ 0 & 0 & 0.700 \\ 0 & 0 & 0.831 \\ 0 & 0 & 0.774 \\ 0 & 0 & 0.849 \\ 0 & 0 & 0.779 \end{bmatrix} \begin{bmatrix} \eta_1 \\ \eta_2 \\ \eta_3 \end{bmatrix} + \begin{bmatrix} 0.518 \\ 0.642 \\ 0.482 \\ 0.555 \\ 0.541 \\ 0.513 \\ 0.577 \\ 0.669 \\ 0.529 \\ 0.448 \\ 0.555 \\ 0.652 \\ 0.490 \\ 0.691 \\ 0.599 \\ 0.720 \\ 0.607 \end{bmatrix} \tag{4-5}
$$

$$
\begin{bmatrix} \eta_1 \\ \eta_2 \\ \eta_3 \end{bmatrix} = \begin{bmatrix} 0 & 0 & 0 \\ 0 & 0 & 0 \\ 0.242 & 0.113 & 0 \end{bmatrix} \begin{bmatrix} \eta_1 \\ \eta_2 \\ \eta_3 \end{bmatrix} + \begin{bmatrix} 0.174 & 0.297 \\ 0.188 & 0.377 \\ 0.043 & 0.408 \end{bmatrix} \begin{bmatrix} \xi_1 \\ \xi_2 \end{bmatrix} + \begin{bmatrix} 0.260 \\ 0.183 \\ 0.448 \end{bmatrix} \qquad (4-6)
$$

4. 5　Discussion

Despite the level and type of agricultural information vary between developing and developed countries, the environmental information greatly influencing the agricultural production and development (Mansell, 2002; Hu et al. , 2006; Harrison and Williams, 2007) . Media play a crucial role to disseminate and promote agricultural technologies, information, and extension service (Burt, 1987) . It also creates awareness and perception through the electronic (radio and television) broadcast, the printing (newspaper, flyers, brochures, and leaflets) outputs, and by the internet to improve the rural agricultural production and development. The empirical standardized structural model result indicates that Media significantly improve the local farmers' land consolidation awareness and perception with the regression coefficient of 0. 25 and 0. 19, respectively. Thus, the results completely support the conceptual framework hypothesis of H1 and H2 of this study. The result demonstrates that Media contribute 25 and 19 percent in the development of awareness and perception of Sichuan smallholder farmers' towards land consolidation, respectively. The contribution of Media to the farmers land consolidation adaptation intention decisions is positive but not significant. The result partially supports the third conceptual framework hypothesis (H3) of this study. Additionally, the total (direct and indirect) effect of Media to land consolidation adaptation intention of farmers is 0. 131. This implies that the overall contribution of Media to perform farmers' land consolidation adaptation intention is only 13 percent. As shown in Figure 11, the short communication materials (flyers, brochures, and leaflets) (X3) plays a greater role in the development of farmers' awareness, perception, and adaptation intentions and followed by electronic (Radio and Television) broadcast (X1), Newspapers (X2) and the Internet (X4), respectively. Dominique and Shanahan (2003) and John and Shanahan (2005) found electronic media (Television) plays a significant and direct effect on farmers agricultural biotechnology adaptations. Therefore, the local government is expected much more works on Media particularly on local Newspaper and the Internet to authorize and promote the efforts of land consolidation and rehabilitation program in rural areas Sichuan province in order to improve the adaptation intention of the local farmers.

In the absence of modern agricultural information communication technologies the farmer to farmer, village to village and district to district agricultural technology dissemination, demonstration, and promotion play a crucial role in the development awareness and perception as well as technology adoptions (Duflo et al. , 2011) . The standardized structural model estimate of the Social – network (ξ_2) with respect to the land consolidation awareness (η_1) and perception (η_2) development of smallholder farmers is positive and highly significant with regression weight of 0. 376 and 0. 334, respectively. The results validate and support the conceptual framework hypothesis H4 and H5 of this study. The result reveals that Social – network contributes 37. 6 percent for awareness and 33. 4 percent for perception development of smallholder farmers' towards land consolidation and rehabilitation program implemented in their village. Moreover, the Social network positive and significantly predict the adaptation intention (η_3) decisions of local farmers on land consolidation. The result highly supports the sixth conceptual framework hypothesis of this study with regression coefficient of 0.44. The result indicates that Social network contributes 44 percent that farmers' to perform land consolidation adaptation intention decisions. Furthermore, the standardized total (direct and indirect) effect of Social network to land consolidation adaptation intention is 0.567 which means implies the overall contribution of Social network that farmers' to perform land consolidation adaptation intention decision is 56.7 percent. In this regard, the relationship between farmers and extension workers (X7) takes the highest share in the development of farmers' land consolidation awareness, perception as well as adaptation intention and followed by relations within the family (X5), the neighbor (X6), and the community (X8), respectively (Figure 6). In general, Social network is a useful tool to disseminate, demonstrate, and promote the efforts of land consolidation and rehabilitation program as well as to improve the individual and collective awareness, perception and adaptation intention decision – making compared to Media ($\xi1$).

Many scholars confirm that the private technology adaptation is not only influenced by the availability of information communication technology and social relations but also by the technical know – how, ability, attitude, perception, sensitivity, consciousness and understanding of individual's themselves (Hassan and Nhemachena, 2008; Bryan et al., 2009; Deressa et al., 2009, 2011; Below et al., 2012). The standardized structural model result showed the individual land consolidation awareness ($\eta1$) and perception ($\eta2$) has a positive and significant influence that farmer's to perform land consolidation adaptation intention ($\eta3$) decisions with estimation coefficient of 0.21 and 0.14, respectively. The results validate and support the H7 and H8 conceptual framework hypotheses of this study. The result reveals that when farmers aware and perceived of land consolidation and rehabilitation program implementing in their village their adaptation intentions improve by 20 and 14 percent, respectively. Many researchers confirm risk perception and attitude of climate change information significantly affect the farmers' climate change adaptation intention (Sharifzadeh et al. , 2012; Kumar, 2012; Arbuckle et al. , 2015) . Therefore, distinguishing the private awareness and perception of land consolidation is very crucial to understand the adaptation intention decision – making of smallholder farmers in Sichuan province, China.

The above results validate and support the conceptual framework model and hypothesis of the study in which all of the seven estimates of path coefficient are statistically significant except Media ($\xi1$) . The signs of all the path coefficients are also as expected. The squared multiple correlations (R^2) are 0. 44 for our targeted land consolidation adaptation intention. The result implies that 44 percent of farmers' land consolidation adaptation intention decisions can be explained by the conceptual framework of this study.

4. 6 Conclusion

China has investing large amount of manpower, material, and financial resources in Rural Land Consolidation (RLC) program and achieving a remarkable results in reclaiming poor quality soils, reducing land fragmentation, improving of agricultural infrastructures, and building clean and tidy villages through partner – based and participatory approach, particularly in many rural areas of Sichuan province. This study adopt the Theory of Planned Behavior (TPB) and utilize the Structural Equation Modeling (SEM) technique aimed to examine the contribution of Media and Social network in the development of farmers' land consolidation awareness, perception, and adaptation intention in Sichuan Province, China. This research work generates information to authorize and promote the efforts of land consolidation and rehabilitation program in order to improve the farmers' adaptation intention of land consolidation and achieve sustainable agricultural production in rural areas of Sichuan province. According to SEM – CFA model fit criterion the overall model goodness – of – fit of the constructed conceptual framework of this study are ideal and no model modification was done. The findings of the standardized structural model estimate of this study indicated that Social network plays a significant role in the development of farmers' awareness, perception as well as adaptation intentions of land consolidation. The total (direct and indirect) effect of Social network to perform farmers' land consolidation adaptation intention decisions is 56 percent. The contribution of Media in the developments of farmers' awareness and perception is significant, while, to the farmers' LC adaptation intention is insignificant. The total (direct and indirect) effect of Media to perform farmers' land consolidation adaptation intention is quite poor (13%) compare to Social network. The short communication materials (flyers, brochures and leaflets) are play key role in the development of farmers' awareness, perception, and adaptation intention decisions and followed by Electronic (Radio and Television) broadcast, local Newspapers and the Internet. Hence, our results conclude that Social network is a useful tool to dissemination, demonstration, and promotion the efforts of land consolidation and rehabilitation program as well as to improve the individual and collective awareness, perception and adaptation intention decision – making than Media. In addition, when farmers aware and perceived of land consolidation and rehabilitation program implemented in their village the adaptation intention decisions to use agricultural inputs such as fertilizer, improved seed, and machinery significantly improved.

Thus, the local government authority is much more expected to use Media particularly the local Newspapers and the Internet to authorize and promote the efforts of land consolidation and rehabilitation program in rural areas of Sichuan province as well as to improve the awareness, perception, and adaptation intention rural Sichuan farmers.

V. The Perspectives and Adaptive Intention of Land Fragmentation in Ethiopia: The Case of Amhara Region Smallholder Farmers

5.1 Introduction

   The majority of the Ethiopian agricultural economy is dominated by small – scaled rural farming system. And the agricultural land continues as key livelihood and financial security as well as profound as people's living standard, wealth, social status and aspirations indicator of rural areas of Ethiopia. However, due to rapid population growth, land degradation, urbanization and industrial development, agricultural land become a scarce resource in the country (USAID, 2004; Belay et al. , 2005; ERSS, 2013).

   The country has been undergoing tremendous land laws and reforms to improve land use and land tenure system to increase productivity, thus contributing to the growth and transformation of the agricultural production as well as the transition to urbanization and industrialization. These land laws and reforms are also acknowledged hundreds of thousands of peasants to own lands through quick and massive land re/distribution system. The land re/distribution system in Ethiopia has been done by local peasant associations (PA's) based on their family size, land and soil quality (slope, fertility, distance), and agro – ecology. In spite of the remarkable and quick land re/distribution, the one side consequence of the land re/distribution is land fragmentation and has become crucial issues and more challenging with detrimental implications for private and public investments, sustainable economic growth, social and natural resources development.

Agricultural land fragmentation is a common phenomenon in Ethiopia, particularly in the Central Highlands of Ethiopia (Amhara region) and affects the agricultural production systems. According to the ERSS (2013) report a farm household is cultivating 11 farm parcels with an average size of 0. 23 ha in the study region (Amhara region) . These farm parcels have also different land characteristics. For example, different soil fertility classes such as "lem", "lem – tef", "tef" (for fertile, moderately fertile and infertile soils), different topographic (slope) classes such as "medama", "dagetama" and "gedel" (for flat, gentle and steep slope), different shapes, distance from home, access to irrigation and road.

Many studies have indicated that land fragmentation is a major threat to agricultural production because it hinders modern agricultural mechanization, obstacle to install agricultural infrastructures (such as irrigation and drainage system, road network), cause land and soil degradation problems, impede to equal and frequent follow – up and management, increase cost of production and consequently cause production inefficiencies as well as production reduction (Nguyen et al. , 1996; Tan et al. , 2008; Studies, 2003; Niroula and Thapa, 2005; Thomas, 2006; Hung et al. , 2007; Di Falco et al., 2010). Bentley (1987) also noted that, land fragmentation involves a complicated boundary network among parcels (hedges, stone walls, ditches, etc.), which causes land wastage as well as conflict on boundaries between neighboring land ownership. In general, all the above problems associated with land fragmentation usually act as an obstacle to rational agricultural development and more explained in Ethiopia. To overcome the impacts and challenges of land fragmentation, many Europeans (Germany, Netherlands, Romania, Cyprus), Asians (China, Japan, India), and Africans (Kenya, Rwanda, Tanzania) countries were implemented land consolidation programs as an alternative land management tool for integrated and sustainable agricultural productions (Thomas, 2006; Rusu, 2002; Demetriou, 2012; Van den Noort, 1987; Huang et al., 2011; Niroula and Thapa, 2005). However, land consolidation is not yet started in Ethiopia while the government encourages voluntary basis.

Studies on farmers' attitude, perceptions and adaptive intentions towards land fragmentation are limited particularly in Ethiopia. Derrese et al. (2011), Yeshineh (2015) and Teshome et al. (2016) used descriptive statistics and Analysis of Variance (ANOVA) to understand farmers' perception of sustainable land management in Ethiopia. However, these models did not indicate the net influence of factors on the response variable and did not distinguish the causal pathways that link cause and effect of the variables. The present study is based on plausible methodological similarities with behavior and psychological studies and adopting of the Theory of Planned Behavior (TPB) and utility of Structural Equation Model (SEM) techniques to fill the gap in the causality relationship as well as the direct and indirect effect of land fragmentation risk perception, adaptation measure, subjective norm and social incentives on farmers' land fragmentation mitigation intentions.

Thus, understanding the private adaptive intention behavior towards land fragmentation in the Ethiopia, particularly in the Central Highlands of Ethiopia is very crucial for Policymakers to plan and implement alternative comprehensive land management tools i. e land consolidation to improve the agricultural production as well as sustainable rural development in the country. Therefore, the purpose of this study is twofold: on the one hand to understand the farmers' perspective and adaptation intention behavior towards land fragmentation in the Central Highlands of Ethiopia; on the other hand, to test the applicability of TPB on land fragmentation adaptive intention through Structural Equation Modeling (SEM) techniques. In addition, this study measure land fragmentation status of the study area and its effect on farmers' adaptive intentions. This study has answered the following research questions: To what extent the farmers' perspectives on land fragmentation risk perception affect their adaptive intention level? To what extent the farmers' adaptation behavior/measures affect their land fragmentation mitigation intention level? And does the social pressure and social incentive affect the farmers land fragmentation mitigation intention?

5. 2 Conceptual framework and research hypothesis

5. 2. 1 Conceptual framework

As shown in Figure 1 this adopts the Theory of Planned Behavior (TPB) model to develop the conceptual framework in order to address the motivation of smallholder farmers towards land fragmentation adaptation intentions for sustainable agricultural production. The constructed conceptual framework this study consists of four exogenous latent variables such as risk perceptions, adaptation behavior/measures, subjective norm and social incentives, four exogenous observed/measured variables (farmland size, number of plots, Simpson's index and Shannon crop diversity index) and one latent endogenous variable (intentions).

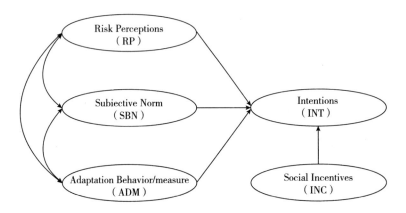

Figure 1   Conceptual framework of the study

5.2.2   Research hypothesis

From the above conceptual framework we have formulated seven research hypotheses. The hypotheses of this study are:

Risk Perception (ξ1): Describes how people assess, look and understand the threats, risks or damage of environmental problem for themselves and others in terms severity, magnitude and frequency according to their risk experience (Witmarsh, 2008; Spence et al., 2011; Dang et al., 2012). When people perceived more about the risk then they develop adaptation measures to cop and reduce the damages and risks. In this study land fragmentation risk perception is an exogenous latent variable that has been subjected into five measured variables (Table 1). Therefore, we hypothesized smallholder farmers that more perceived of land fragmentation risks are more likely to adaptive intentions (H1) .

Subjective Norm ($\xi 2$) : Subjective norm can be comprehended as the perceived social force/pressure to engage/performing or not engage/performing in a particular behavior (Ajzen, 1991; Kaufmann et al. , 2009) . The land fragmentation adaptation intention pressure might come from family members, neighbor or farmers group (cell), the extension agents and the community. In this study, subjective norm is an exogenous latent variable that has been measured by four observed variables. Hence, we hypothesized smallholder farmers that more perceived of social pressure are expected more expected to adaptive intentions (H2) .

Adaptation Behavior/Measure ($\xi 3$) : Adaptation is the dynamic process of which the behavior and psychological mechanism of an individual continually change to adjust the variations in living conditions and environment to improve their survival (Kaufmann et al. , 2009; Dang et al. , 2012, 2014) . Farmers that have perceived of land fragmentation risks and social pressure might help them to implement adaptation measures to reduce the risks and damages. In this research paper, adaptation measure is an exogenous latent variable that has been subjected into four observed variables (Table 1) . Hence, we hypothesized smallholder farmers that performing adaptive measures are highly motivated to mitigate land fragmentation risks (H3) .

Social Incentives ($\xi 4$) : Social incentives are community based infrastructural development activities such as: (a) environmental protection program (terracing, plantation) in terms of cash, kind, cost sharing or free; (b) access to market and rural bank/credit centers; (c) access to extension service centers (agriculture, health, school) . These social incentives might be motivate the smallholder farmers for better production as well as resource management and protection. In our conceptual framework the social incentive is an exogenous latent variable that has been measured by three observed variable. Consequently, we hypothesized that smallholder farmers perceived of social incentives are more motivated to adaptation intentions (H4).

Farmland Size (K1): It is an exogenous observed variable used to identify the relationship between total farmland holding size of the households and their adaptive intention towards land fragmentation. Therefore, in this study we expected an inverse relationship between farm size and adaptation intention that is farmers having large farmland size are less – likely to intend land fragmentation mitigation measures (H5).

Number of plots (K2): It is one of the land fragmentation indicators that indicate how much farm plots are owned by a single farmer. In this research paper K2 is an exogenous observed variable used to indicate to measure the effect of plot numbers on the farmers' intention to mitigate land fragmentation. Hence, we hypothesized that smallholder farmers having more number of plots are more intend to mitigation measures (H6).

Simpson index (K3): This index used to measure the land fragmentation status of the farm household and calculated by equation 3 as indicated in Chapter two. Its value ranges between 0 and 1 and an index closer to zero is less fragmented and vice – verse. In this study K3 an exogenous observed variable used to estimate the effect of land fragmentation on smallholder farmers mitigation intention. Thus, we hypothesized smallholder farmers having higher Simpson index are the more intend to mitigate land fragmentation (H7).

Shannon Index (K4): it measures the diversification crops and their relative abundance (land allocation among crops) (Shannon, 1948). Shannon index is calculated using equation 15 and its value equals zero if there is only one crop (i. e. no diversity) and increases with the number of cultivated crops. In this study K4 is an exogenous observed variable that is used to predict its effect on the smallholder farmers land fragmentation adaptation intentions. Thus, we expected that the higher SH value are the less intentions to land fragmentation mitigation (H8).

$$SH = \sum (p_i \times \ln p_i) \qquad\qquad (5-1)$$

$$P_i = \frac{1}{j} \qquad\qquad (5-2)$$

Where, P_i is the share of the area covered by a specific crop, and J is the maximum possible number of crops cultivated.

Intentions/motivation ($\eta 5$): Intention assesses what the farmers' want to practice, achieve or to devise in the future as well as their final desire/goal (Ajzen, 1991; Kaufmann et al., 2009; Dang et al., 2014). It also helps to develop adaptive strategy to maximize benefit as well as to reduce threats/risks. In this study, intention is an endogenous latent variable that is consider to be influenced by the above exogenous latent and exogenous observed variables. The land fragmentation adaptation has consist of five observed variables (Table 1) which are derived from the principles of land consolidation (Studies, 2003; Thomas, 2006; Demetriou, 2013).

5.3　Research methodology

5.3.1　Variable measurement

To test the research hypotheses and to synthesize the structural link between the latent variables of the conceptual framework, this paper applied the SEM statistical technique. As indicated in the conceptual framework of this study, there are four exogenous independent latent variables and one endogenous dependent latent variable. Further variable setting scale design was developed to make comprehensive measurement of latent variable by their observed variables. Thus, a clear, simple and straightforward land fragmentation structured questionnaire was developed (see Appendix II) that can accurately measure the latent variables of the conceptual framework of the study. The specific dimension of each observed variable are scaled from five Likert scale (Table 1) that reflect sample respondent subjective judgment. The attribute design of each observed variable in the scale is "strongly disagree (1)", "disagree (2)", "uncertain (3)", "agree (4)" and "strongly agree (5)". Whereas, the four exogenous observed variables are scaled continues measurement.

Table 1   Variables used and measurements

Latent variables		Observed variables			Variable measurement
Variable name	Code	Variable name	Code	Description	
Risk Perception	$\eta 1$	Risk Perception 1	X1	Perceived risk of land fragmentation on land degradation and soil erosion	1: Strongly disagree; 2: Disagree; 3: Uncertain; 4: Agree; 5: Strongly agree
		Risk Perception 2	X2	Perceived risk of land fragmentation on to investments in land (inputs use, management) and follow – up activities	
		Risk Perception 3	X3	Perceived risk of land fragmentation on modern agricultural infrastructure and mechanization system	
		Risk Perception 4	X4	Perceived risk of land fragmentation on cost of production (labor, time)	
		Risk Perception 5	X5	Perceived risk of land fragmentation on conflict on the boundary with neighbor land owners	
Subjective Norm	$\eta 2$	Subjective Norm 1	X6	Perceived pressure from family and relatives	1: Strongly disagree; 2: Disagree; 3: Uncertain; 4: Agree; 5: Strongly agree
		Subjective Norm 2	X7	Perceived pressure from neighbor and farmers group (cell) (i. e. one cell has five members)	

Continued Table

Latent variables		Observed variables			Variable measurement
Variable name	Code	Variable name	Code	Description	
Subjective Norm	$\eta 2$	Subjective Norm 3	X8	Perceived pressure from agricultural extension agents	1: Strongly disagree; 2: Disagree; 3: Uncertain; 4: Agree; 5: Strongly agree
		Subjective Norm 4	X9	Perceived pressure from the community members of the village	
Adaptation Behavior/ Measurement	$\eta 3$	Adaptation Behavior 1	X10	Land shared/rent in/out is an adaptive option to reduce land fragmentation risks	1: Strongly disagree; 2: Disagree; 3: Uncertain; 4: Agree; 5: Strongly agree
		Adaptation Behavior 2	X11	Land fallowing practice is an adaptive option to reduce the risks of land fragmentation	
		Adaptation Behavior 3	X12	Land use change (crop land to plantation land) is an alternative adaptive option to reduce the risks of land fragmentation	
		Adaptation Behavior 4	X13	Utilization of farm inputs and management practices are an alternative adaptive option to reduce the risks of land fragmentation	
Social Incentives	$\eta 4$	Social Incentives 1	X14	The land management activities (terracing, planting) in my village encourage for adaptive intentions	1: Strongly disagree; 2: Disagree; 3: Uncertain; 4: Agree; 5: Strongly agree
		Social Incentives 2	X15	Access to the market and bank/credit centers in my village inspire for adaptive intentions	
		Social Incentives 3	X16	Access to the agricultural/health/school services in my village motivate for adaptive intentions	
Intentions/ Motivation	$\eta 5$	Intentions 1	Y1	I always intend to merge and consolidate the scattered farm parcels to larger and better shaped parcel	1: Strongly disagree; 2: Disagree; 3: Uncertain; 4: Agree; 5: Strongly agree
		Intentions 2	Y2	I always intend to have moderate to high quality farm parcel and free of land and soil degradation threats	

Continued Table

| Latent variables | | Observed variables | | | Variable measurement |
Variable name	Code	Variable name	Code	Description	
Intentions/ Motivation	η5	Intentions 3	Y3	I always intend to have access to irrigation and drainage system and road network in my parcels	1: Strongly disagree; 2: Disagree; 3: Uncertain; 4: Agree; 5: Strongly agree
		Intentions 4	Y4	I always intend to use modern agricultural mechanization	
		Intentions 5	Y5	I always intend to use the recommended farm inputs (fertilizer, variety, seed rate) for better production	
Observed variables		Farm size	K1	Farm size holding of the household	>0
		Number of plots	K2	The number of farm plot holding of the households	>0
		Simpsons index	K3	The land fragmentation status of the farm household	0 - 1
		Shannon index	K4	The crop diversification system of the household	≥0

5. 3. 2 Estimation procedure

In this study the Confirmatory Factor Analysis (CFA) has been subjected to Maximum Likelihood Estimate (MLE) to capture the models Goodness – of – Fit (GOF) and run by means of International Business Machine – Analysis of Moment structure (IBM – AMOS) version 22. 0.

As discussed in Chapter three the conceptual framework of the measurement and structural models and equation (5 – 3), equation (5 – 4) and equation (5 – 5) which can be expressed in matrix form for the following mathematical model.

$$
\begin{bmatrix} x_1 \\ x_2 \\ x_3 \\ x_4 \\ x_5 \\ x_6 \\ x_7 \\ x_8 \\ x_9 \\ x_{10} \\ x_{11} \\ x_{12} \\ x_{13} \\ x_{14} \\ x_{15} \\ x_{16} \end{bmatrix} =
\begin{bmatrix}
\lambda_{x1} & 0 & 0 & 0 \\
\lambda_{x2} & 0 & 0 & 0 \\
\lambda_{x3} & 0 & 0 & 0 \\
\lambda_{x4} & 0 & 0 & 0 \\
\lambda_{x5} & 0 & 0 & 0 \\
0 & \lambda_{x6} & 0 & 0 \\
0 & \lambda_{x7} & 0 & 0 \\
0 & \lambda_{x8} & 0 & 0 \\
0 & \lambda_{x9} & 0 & 0 \\
0 & 0 & \lambda_{x10} & 0 \\
0 & 0 & \lambda_{x11} & 0 \\
0 & 0 & \lambda_{x12} & 0 \\
0 & 0 & \lambda_{x13} & 0 \\
0 & 0 & 0 & \lambda_{x14} \\
0 & 0 & 0 & \lambda_{x15} \\
0 & 0 & 0 & \lambda_{x16}
\end{bmatrix}
\begin{bmatrix} \eta_1 \\ \eta_2 \\ \eta_3 \\ \eta_4 \end{bmatrix} +
\begin{bmatrix} \delta_1 \\ \delta_2 \\ \delta_3 \\ \delta_4 \\ \delta_5 \\ \delta_6 \\ \delta_7 \\ \delta_8 \\ \delta_9 \\ \delta_{10} \\ \delta_{11} \\ \delta_{12} \\ \delta_{13} \\ \delta_{14} \\ \delta_{15} \\ \delta_{16} \end{bmatrix}
\qquad (5-3)
$$

$$
\begin{bmatrix} y_1 \\ y_2 \\ y_3 \\ y_4 \\ y_5 \end{bmatrix} =
\begin{bmatrix} \lambda_{y1} \\ \lambda_{y2} \\ \lambda_{y3} \\ \lambda_{y4} \\ \lambda_{y5} \end{bmatrix}
\begin{bmatrix} \eta_5 \end{bmatrix} +
\begin{bmatrix} \varepsilon_1 \\ \varepsilon_2 \\ \varepsilon_3 \\ \varepsilon_4 \\ \varepsilon_5 \end{bmatrix}
\qquad (5-4)
$$

$$
\begin{bmatrix} \eta_5 \end{bmatrix} = \begin{bmatrix} \beta_{5,1} & \beta_{5,2} & \beta_{5,3} & \beta_{5,4} & \beta_{5,5} & \beta_{5,6} & \beta_{5,7} & \beta_{5,8} \end{bmatrix} \begin{bmatrix} \eta_5 \end{bmatrix} + \begin{bmatrix} \zeta_1 \end{bmatrix}
\qquad (5-5)
$$

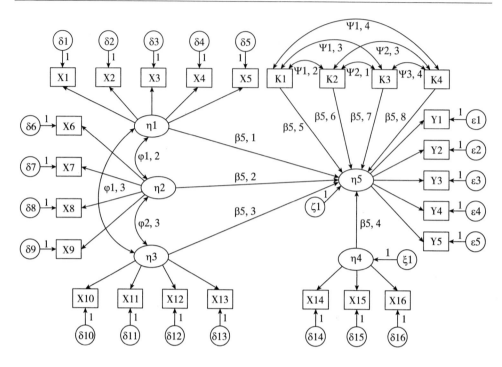

Figure 2   Land fragmentation adaptation intention model

5. 4   Results

5. 4. 1   Descriptive statistics of the respondent

The snapshot descriptive statistics of the sample farm household is presented in Table 2. The result showed that the male headed household are 89. 1% whereas the female headed households are 10. 9%. This implies that the male headed farm households are dominating in the study area than female headed. The age of the respondents are range between 18 and 80 years old with average age 45 years. The higher age distribution of the respondents are found in the range of 41 to 60 years old (49.1%), followed by 18 –40 years old (41.0%) and the remaining 9.9% are 61 –80 years old. In addition, the farming experience of the samples are range between 3 and 63 years, with average of 28 years' experience. Further, more than 52% of the respondents have 10 to 40% farming experience. The majority of the respondents (93.3%) are able to read and write and attended primary and above school whereas the remaining 6.7% are illiterate. The highest number of family member distribution (60.2%) is found between 4 to 6 members. The average household family size is 5 and 60% of them are actively participating in farming activities such as ploughing, weeding, harvesting, trashing and transporting. Based on the local wealth standard the sample farmers were indicated themselves their wealth status; accordingly, 70.4 respondents are categorized in moderate and 19.3% grouped in richest while the remaining 10.3% are grouped in poor. According to the ERSS 2013 report, the average rural household family size of the study region is 4.6. The average farmland holding size per household was 1.42ha, with average number and size of parcel of 6.2 plots 0.23 ha, respectively. This indicates that the land holding size of the study area is lower than the regional average (1.8ha). More than 85% of the respondents are farming 4 and above farm plots. The average numbers of farm plots per household at regional level are 11 parcels with average parcel size of 0.23 ha (ERSS, 2013).

Table 2　Descriptive statistics of the sample farm households' result

Variables	Groups	Frequency	Percent	Std. D.
Sex	Male	361	89.1	0.312
	Female	44	10.9	
Age	18 –40	166	41.0	0.643
	41 –60	199	49.1	
	61 –80	40	9.9	

Continued Table

Variables	Groups	Frequency	Percent	Std. D.
Education level	Illiterate	27	6. 7	
	Grade 1 – 4	265	65. 4	
	Grade 5 – 8	85	21. 0	0. 689
	Grade 9 – 12	28	6. 9	
Farming Experience	< 10 years	46	11. 4	
	11 – 20 years	107	26. 4	
	21 – 30 years	106	26. 2	1. 467
	31 – 40 years	78	19. 3	
	40 – 63 years	68	16. 8	
Family members	1 – 3	79	19. 5	
	4 – 6	244	60. 2	0. 631
	6 – 11	82	20. 2	
Family labor	1 – 2	215	53. 1	
	3 – 4	154	38. 0	0. 652
	5 – 9	36	8. 9	
Wealth status (local standard)	Poor	42	10. 3	
	Moderate	285	70. 4	0. 543
	Rich	78	19. 3	
Land holding size	< 0. 5ha	53	13. 1	
	0. 5 – 1. 0ha	112	27. 7	
	1. 0 – 1. 5ha	100	24. 7	1. 338
	1. 5 – 2. 0ha	67	16. 5	
	2. 0 – 3. 0ha	65	16. 0	
	3. 0 – 4. 75ha	8	2. 0	
Number of farm plots	1 – 3	57	14. 1	
	4 – 6	184	45. 4	
	7 – 9	119	29. 4	0. 908
	10 – 12	37	9. 1	
	12 – 16	8	2. 0	

Note: Total number of farm household sample (N = 405) .

In summary, the standard deviation among the sample farm household indicates mostly less than 1 which implies that there is less variation in the sample farmers. The descriptive statistical analysis result more importantly ensure the reliability and validity of the individual sample has a good representation, through the individual characteristics of a comprehensive reflection of the sample. Therefore, the sample farm household data can be used for empirical analysis of structural equation model to test the hypothesis of land fragmentation adaptation intentions proposed in this chapter to verify the theoretical model.

5.4.2 Descriptive statistics of model variables

The descriptive statistics of the 25 model observed variables of 405 sample individual is run by means of SPSS 22.0 statistical software and is presented in Table 3. The statistical results show that the mean level of land fragmentation risk perception of the respondents are range between 3.93 to 3.99 with the overall mean risk perception of score of 3.96. The result revealed that, smallholder farmers are more perceived of land fragmentation risks in their village. The average minimum and maximum score of Subjective norm observed variables are 4.24 and 4.30 respectively. The total mean score of the latent subjective norm variable is 4.27 which implies that smallholder farmers of the study area are more perceived of social pressure for their family, farmers group, extension agents and the community. The average adaptation behavior score of smallholder farmers towards land fragmentation 3.44 with minimum and maximum observed variables score of 3.31 and 3.65. Thus, compared to other latent variables of this study the adaptation behavior score of the smallholder farmers on land fragmentation is low. The maximum and minimum score of social incentives observed variables are 4.17 and 4.15, respectively, with mean latent score of 4.16. In addition, the land fragmentation adaptation intention observed variables score range from 4. 27 to 4. 40. The overall adaptation intention latent variable score of the respondents are 4. 36 which is higher than the other latent variables of this study. The result demonstrated that, smallholder farmers are more intended to mitigate land fragmentation. From the standard deviation perspectives, the standard deviations of all observed variables are in the range of 0. 43 to 1. 18. The higher standard deviation was found in the adaptation behavior latent variable whereas the smallest standard deviation found in social incentive latent variable. The higher level of agreement for all observed variables and latent variables were 5 (strongly agree) whereas the minimum level of agreement is for adaptation behavior variables 1 (strongly disagree) . The higher mode value is 4 (agree) is found in all latent variables except in adaptation behavior 2 (disagree) . However, the median level of all latent variables and their observed variables were 4 (agree) .

The descriptive statistics of exogenous observed variables used for land fragmentation adaptation intention model also presented in Table 3. The result showed that the minimum and maximum land holding size are 4. 75 and 0. 13 ha, respectively. The average number of farm plots per household is 6. 23 plots. The average land fragmentation index according to Simpson index is 0. 76 which demonstrated that the study area is severely affected by land fragmentation. In addition, smallholder farmers of the study area were diversify crops along their fragmented farm plots. The average Shannon crop diversity index of the respondents are 0. 92 which is quite high. The overall descriptive statistics result showed that, the data has a good representation, indicating that the variables set in this research are more reasonable. Thus, all the research variables selected in this paper can be used for the structural equation measurement model to meet the needs of building the conceptual model and empirical model of the structural equation of land consolidation adaptation intention.

Table 3　Descriptive statistics of the variables

Latent variables		Observed variables		Max	Min	Mode	Median	Mean	S. D
Variable name	Code	Variable name	Code						
Risk Perception	η1	Risk Perception 1	X1	5	2	4	4	3. 93	0. 96
		Risk Perception 2	X2	5	2	4	4	3. 95	0. 99
		Risk Perception 3	X3	5	2	4	4	3. 94	0. 96
		Risk Perception 4	X4	5	2	4	4	3. 99	0. 89
		Risk Perception 5	X5	5	2	4	4	3. 99	0. 85
Subjective Norm	η2	Subjective Norm 1	X6	5	3	4	4	4. 28	0. 47
		Subjective Norm 2	X7	5	3	4	4	4. 26	0. 47
		Subjective Norm 3	X8	5	2	4	4	4. 24	0. 46
		Subjective Norm 4	X9	5	3	4	4	4. 30	0. 46
Adaptation Measure	η3	Adaptation Behavior 1	X10	5	1	2	4	3. 39	1. 18
		Adaptation Behavior 2	X11	5	1	4	4	3. 40	1. 15
		Adaptation Behavior 3	X12	5	1	2	4	3. 31	1. 20
		Adaptation Behavior 4	X13	5	1	4	4	3. 65	1. 05
Social Incentives	η4	Social Incentives 1	X14	5	2	4	4	4. 15	0. 45
		Social Incentives 2	X15	5	2	4	4	4. 17	0. 43
		Social Incentives 3	X16	5	2	4	4	4. 16	0. 44
Intention / Motivation	η5	Intention 1	Y1	5	3	4	4	4. 39	0. 53
		Intention 2	Y2	5	4	4	4	4. 40	0. 49
		Intention 3	Y3	5	3	4	4	4. 35	0. 51
		Intention 4	Y4	5	3	4	4	4. 27	0. 50
		Intention 5	Y5	5	3	4	4	4. 38	0. 51
Observed exogenous variables		Farm size	K1	4. 75	0. 13	1. 0	1. 25	1. 42	0. 77
		Number of plots	K2	16	1	6	6	6. 23	2. 60
		Simpsons index	K3	0. 92	0. 0	0. 75	0. 79	0. 76	0. 11
		Shannon index	K4	1. 85	0. 0	0. 69	1. 01	0. 92	0. 040

5. 4. 3　Data adequacy, consistency and validity checking

Sample data adequacy, internal consistency and validity measurement is very essential prior of structural equation model estimation (Teguh, 2007; Hair et al. ,

2010）. Thus, in this study, the sample adequacy, consistency and validity was assessed using Kaiser – Meyer – Olkin (KMO) and the Bartlett test of Sphericity, Cronbach's alpha (α), determinant value, factor loading (λ), Composite Reliability (CR), and Average Variance Extracted (AVE) and correlation matric by means of SPSS 22. 0 statistical package.

5. 4. 3. 1 Data validity result

The suitability of the data for model development was evaluated using the Kaiser – Meyer – Olkin (KMO) and Bartlett's test of sphericity and the result is presented in Table 4. The results shows that, the KMO indexes of the latent variables range between 0. 728 and 0. 876 which are above the minimum KMO threshold value of 0. 5. Thus, the result demonstrated there is sufficient data available for factor analysis (Kaiser, 1974; Hair et al. , 2010). In addition, the results of Bartlett's test of sphericity result showed approximate chi – square (χ^2) value of 4660, a degree of freedom of 210 and highly significant at p < 0. 0001 significant level which indicated the sample data was appropriate for factor analysis. Thus, the overall data validity checking result demonstrated that the surveyed data for SEM development are adequate (Hair et al. , 2010).

Table 4 Data adequacy and suitability result

Latent variables		Observed variables		KMO	Bartlett's Test		
Variable name	Code	Variable name	Code		χ^2	DF	Sig.
Risk Perception	η1	Risk Perception 1	X1	0. 876	1303. 00	10	***
		Risk Perception 2	X2				
		Risk Perception 3	X3				
		Risk Perception 4	X4				
		Risk Perception 5	X5				

Continued Table

Latent variables		Observed variables		KMO	Bartlett's Test		
Variable name	Code	Variable name	Code		χ^2	DF	Sig.
Subjective Norm	η2	Subjective Norm 1	X6	0. 798	532. 87	6	∗∗∗
		Subjective Norm 2	X7				
		Subjective Norm 3	X8				
		Subjective Norm 4	X9				
Adaptation Measure	η3	Adaptation Behavior 1	X10	0. 805	851. 10	6	∗∗∗
		Adaptation Behavior 2	X11				
		Adaptation Behavior 3	X12				
		Adaptation Behavior 4	X13				
Social Incentives	η4	Social Incentives 1	X14	0. 728	789. 72	3	∗∗∗
		Social Incentives 2	X15				
		Social Incentives 3	X16				
Intention/ Motivation	η5	Intention 1	Y1	0. 856	860. 59	10	∗∗∗
		Intention 2	Y2				
		Intention 3	Y3				
		Intention 4	Y4				
		Intention 5	Y5				
Entire variables				0. 840	4660. 00	210	∗∗∗

Note: ∗∗∗ Significant at $p < 0.0001$ significance level.

5. 4. 3. 2 Data reliability results

The reliability and internal consistency among observed variables comprising constructed variable was estimated using Cronbach's alpha. The Cronbach's alpha result and determinant value are presented in Table 5. The result indicated that, the Cronbach's alpha value of observed variables are range between 0. 810 to 0. 823 and 0. 815 to 0. 909 for latent constructs. Thus, the Cronbach's alpha value of observed and latent variables are above the minimum cutoff value of 0. 7 (Lyubomirsky and Lepper, 1999; Hair et al. , 2010) . In addition, the Cronbach's alphas of the observed variables are less than their respective latent constructs. The result demonstrated that, there was no need to remove observed variables from their respective latent variables. Further, the determinant value of the each latent constructs and the model is greater than the cutoff value of 0. 0000001 (Table 5). Thus, the result indicated that there is no multicollinearity and computational problem for the factor analysis (Field, 2009). Thus, the overall data reliability checking result demonstrated that the surveyed data for SEM development are reliable and internally consistent (Hair et al., 2010).

Table 5　Data reliability and consistency of measurement of the constructs

Latent variables		Observed variables		Cronbach's	Determinant
Variable name	Code	Variable name	Code	Alpha (α)	values
Risk Perception	η1	Risk Perception 1	X1	0. 811	
		Risk Perception 2	X2	0. 813	
		Risk Perception 3	X3	0. 814	0. 909	0. 039
		Risk Perception 4	X4	0. 810	
		Risk Perception 5	X5	0. 816	
Subjective Norm	η2	Subjective Norm 1	X6	0. 822	
		Subjective Norm 2	X7	0. 821	0. 815	0. 266
		Subjective Norm 3	X8	0. 821	
		Subjective Norm 4	X9	0. 823	
Adaptation Measure	η3	Adaptation Behavior 1	X10	0. 816	
		Adaptation Behavior 2	X11	0. 822	0. 878	0. 120
		Adaptation Behavior 3	X12	0. 813	
		Adaptation Behavior 4	X13	0. 814	
Social Incentives	η4	Social Incentives 1	X14	0. 823	
		Social Incentives 2	X15	0. 822	0. 898	0. 140
		Social Incentives 3	X16	0. 822	
Intention / Motivation	η5	Intention 1	Y1	0. 820	
		Intention 2	Y2	0. 821	
		Intention 3	Y3	0. 819	0. 863	0. 117
		Intention 4	Y4	0. 821	
		Intention 5	Y5	0. 821	
Model				**0. 818**	**0. 826**	**0. 000008**

5. 4. 3. 3 Factor loading, Composite Reliability (CR), Average Variance Extracted (AVE) results

The factor loading result indicates the relationship of the observed items to their associated constructs (factors) and contributes to validity check (Hair et al. , 2010) . The average factor loading of the construct are ranging between 0. 713 and 0. 863 which are above the minimum cutoff value of 0. 7 and statistically significant at 0. 001 significance level. The standardized factor loading of the observed items should be at least 0. 5 and statistically significant (Hair et al. , 2010) . Our result showed (Table 6) that the factor loading of the observed items are ranges from 0. 638 to 0. 910. Hence, the observed variables of this study are strongly correlated to their latent variables thus, the overall factor loading result validates the conceptual framework latent constructs are explained by their observed variables.

In addition, the Composite Reliability (CR) and Average Variance Extracted (AVE) of the five latent variables are presented in Table 6. The result shows that the CR value of the latent constructs are range between 0. 817 and 0. 910 which are above the minimum CR threshold of 0. 7. Thus, the CR result indicates that the degree to which the observed variables explain the latent construct is reliable and support to proceed factor analysis. The minimum and maximum AVE values of the latent variables are 0. 557 and 0. 753, respectively. The AVE values of the latent constructs are above the minimum cutoff value of 0. 5. The results demonstrated that, the amount of variance captured by construct through its items (observed variables) in comparison to the amount of variance captured due to the measurement error is minimum (Fornell and Larcker, 1981; Bagozzi and Yi, 1988; Hair et al. , 2010) . Thus, the there is no convergence concern between the latent constructs and observed variables to proceed factor analysis.

Table 6 Factors Loading （λ）, Composite Reliability

（CR）, Average Variance Extracted （AVE）

Latent variables		Observed variables		Factors Loading （λ）	CR	AVE
Variable name	Code	Variable name	Code			
Risk Perception	η1	Risk Perception 1	X1	0. 883[a]	0. 910	0. 668
		Risk Perception 2	X2	0. 787 ***		
		Risk Perception 3	X3	0. 830 ***		
		Risk Perception 4	X4	0. 788 ***		
		Risk Perception 5	X5	0. 786 ***		
Subjective Norm	η2	Subjective Norm 1	X6	0. 638 ***	0. 817	0. 529
		Subjective Norm 2	X7	0. 810[a]		
		Subjective Norm 3	X8	0. 707 ***		
		Subjective Norm 4	X9	0. 697 ***		
Adaptation Measure	η3	Adaptation Behavior 1	X10	0. 846[a]	0. 879	0. 645
		Adaptation Behavior 2	X11	0. 752 ***		
		Adaptation Behavior 3	X12	0. 781 ***		
		Adaptation Behavior 4	X13	0. 822 ***		
Social Incentives	η4	Social Incentives 1	X14	0. 776 ***	0. 901	0. 753
		Social Incentives 2	X15	0. 904 ***		
		Social Incentives 3	X16	0. 910[a]		
Intention / Motivation	η5	Intention 1	Y1	0. 738[a]	0. 862	0. 557
		Intention 2	Y2	0. 668 ***		
		Intention 3	Y3	0. 725 ***		
		Intention 4	Y4	0. 763 ***		
		Intention 5	Y5	0. 780 ***		

5. 4. 3. 4 Discriminant and convergent validity

According to Fornell and Larcker （1981）, the discriminant validity test result of the latent variables is assessed by comparing the square root of AVE （SQR – AVE） value and their correlation coefficients. They suggest that if the SQR – AVE value is greater than the correlation coefficient, thus, there is no discriminant concern to precede factor analysis and develop the model. The correlation matrix among the latent variables is positive and statistically significant (Table 7). The higher correlation coefficient was found between subjective norm and intention/motivation latent variables (0.45) and followed by social incentives and intention/motivation latent variables (0.33) and statistically significant at 1%. While the minimum correlation was found between risk perception and subjective norm (0.102) but significant at 10% significant level. Further, the square root of AVE value among latent variable is greater than the inter - constructs correlation coefficient. The result validated that, there is no discriminant concern to proceed factor analysis and develop model (Hair et al. , 2010; Malhotra and Dash, 2011).

Table 7   Discriminant validity test result

Latent variables		Risk Perception	Subjective Norm	Adaptation Measure	Social Incentives	Intention/ Motivation
		$\eta 1$	$\eta 2$	$\eta 3$	$\eta 4$	$\eta 5$
Risk Perception	$\eta 1$	0. 817				
Subjective Norm	$\eta 2$	0. 102 (0. 010)†	0. 72			
Adaptation Measure	$\eta 3$	0. 178 (0. 032) **	0. 203 (0. 041) ***	0. 803		
Social Incentives	$\eta 4$	0. 118 (0. 014) *	0. 307 (0. 094) ***	0. 115 (0. 013) *	0. 868	
Intention / Motivation	$\eta 5$	0. 172 (0. 029) **	0. 447 (0. 200) ***	0. 116 (0. 013) *	0. 327 (0. 107) ***	0. 746

Note: $\dagger$ p < 0. 1, * = p < 0. 05, ** = p < 0. 01, *** = p < 0. 001; The diagonal values shown in bold text indicate the square root of AVE and the others are the correlation matrix with square correlation in parentheses.

The standardized and unstandardized path coefficient of the measurement model latent variables to their corresponding observed variables presented in Table 8. The result shows that the standardized estimation coefficient of latent variables to observed variables found in the range of 0. 649 to 0. 923 and significant at 0. 0001 level. The critical ratios (C. R.) value of all the observed variables are in the range of 12. 5 to 25. 0 which are greater than the C. R. minimum standard (C. R. > 3. 28) . The result revealed that, all the observed variables are converge to their corresponding latent variables, and all the latent variables have good explanatory power for their observed indicators.

Table 8　Standardized and unstandardized path coefficient of land
fragmentation adaptation intention measurement model

Path relationship	Unstandardized estimate	S. E.	C. R.	P – value	Standardized estimate
X1←η1	1	—	—	—	0. 884
X2←η1	0. 925	0. 047	19. 668	＊＊＊	0. 787
X3←η1	0. 932	0. 044	21. 386	＊＊＊	0. 827
X4←η1	0. 852	0. 042	20. 501	＊＊＊	0. 807
X5←η1	0. 782	0. 041	19. 296	＊＊＊	0. 778
X6←η2	0. 792	0. 063	12. 497	＊＊＊	0. 649
X7←η2	1	—	—	—	0. 818
X8←η2	0. 854	0. 062	13. 693	＊＊＊	0. 710
X9←η2	0. 869	0. 062	13. 923	＊＊＊	0. 723
X10←η3	1	—	—	—	0. 843
X11←η3	0. 847	0. 053	16. 027	＊＊＊	0. 732
X12←η3	0. 965	0. 053	18. 055	＊＊＊	0. 802
X13←η3	0. 881	0. 047	18. 867	＊＊＊	0. 832
X14←η4	0. 862	0. 044	19. 418	＊＊＊	0. 768
X15←η4	0. 998	0. 04	24. 999	＊＊＊	0. 923
X16←η4	1	—	—	—	0. 905
Y11←η5	1. 078	0. 077	14. 048	＊＊＊	0. 753
Y12←η5	1	0. 071	14. 028	＊＊＊	0. 752
Y13←η5	1. 058	0. 074	14. 283	＊＊＊	0. 767
Y14←η5	0. 995	0. 073	13. 634	＊＊＊	0. 730
Y15←η5	1	—	—	—	0. 728

Note: ＊＊＊ is significant at P < 0. 0001, S. E is standard error, C. R. is Critical Ratio.

Generally, the pre – SEM model estimation survey data checking results such as Cronbach's alpha, KMO, determinant value, factor loading, CR, AVE, Correlation matrix and SQR – AVE of the observed items and their associate latent constructs are at an acceptable range and support to precede factor analysis and develop the model. Therefore, the next step is determining the structural model Goodness – of – Fit (GoF) indexes for factor analysis using Maximum Likelihood Estimate.

5.4.4 Confirmatory factor analysis (CFA) results

Since, the sample data reliability, consistency and validity of the observed items their associate construct variables are in an acceptable range and support to proceed factor analysis and develop the model, the next step is checking the model Goodness – of – Fit (GOF) indexes and determining the structural model factor analysis by means of IBM – AMOS 22.0 statistical package.

5.4.4.1 Model goodness of fit checking

The model goodness of fit (GOF) result of structural model is presented in Table 9. The chi – square is 440.74 and statistically significant and normed chi – square is 1.68 which is less than the upper acceptable threshold (CMIN/df < 3.0). Thus the o-verall Chi – square indexes are ideal (Kline, 1998; Hair et al., 2010). The absolute fit indexes are above the minimum standard criteria of GOF. The GFI and AGFI are 0.919 and 0.900 respectively, which are above the recommended acceptable threshold value of 0.90 (Hair et al., 2010). The results demonstrated that the conceptual framework of this study is strongly fit (Chau and Hu, 2001; Hair et al., 2010). The RMSEA, RMR and SRMR values of the structural model are 0.041, 0.039 and 0.063 which are within the standard acceptable cutoff values of 0.08, 0.05 and 0.01, re-spectively. The results revealed that, the difference between the observed correlation and predicted correlation is ideal. In addition, the incremental indexes such as NFI, IFI, TLI and CFI are above the standard values. The results demonstrated that, the constructed conceptual framework of this study ideal and high degree of correlation among model variables and good degree of fit between the research framework and the data (Gerbing and Anderson, 1992; Hair et al., 2010). Generally, according to the model fit indexes requirement, the overall structural model results are at acceptable ranges and indicate that there is a good degree of fit between the research framework and the data. Therefore, following to Hair et al. (2010) suggestions no model modification was required to improve the model fit.

Table 9　Structural model goodness of fit result of the land fragmentation model

Model fit indexes criteria			Statistics result	Statistics standards	Remark
Chi – square indexes	Chi – square ((x^2))	CMIN	440. 74	P < 0. 05	Good
	Normed Chi – square	CMIN/df	1. 682	< 3. 00	Good
Absolute fit indexes	Goodness of Fit Index	GFI	0. 919	> 0. 90	Excellent
	Adjusted Goodness of Fit Index	AGFI	0. 900	> 0. 90	Ideal
	Root Mean Square Error Approximation	RMSEA	0. 041	< 0. 08	Excellent
	Root Mean Square Residual	RMR	0. 039	< 0. 05	Excellent
	Standardized Root Mean Square Residual	SRMR	0. 063	< 0. 10	Excellent
Incremental indexes	Normed Fit Index	NFI	0. 915	> 0. 90	Excellent
	Incremental Fit Index	IFI	0. 964	> 0. 90	Excellent
	Tucker Lewis Index	TLI	0. 958	> 0. 90	Excellent
	Comparative Fit Index	CFI	0. 963	> 0. 90	Excellent
Parsimony fit indexes	Parsimony Normed Fit Index	PNFI	0. 799	> 0. 50	Good
	Parsimony Goodness of Fit Index	PGFI	0. 741	> 0. 50	Good
	Parsimony Comparative Fit Index	PCFI	0. 841	> 0. 50	Good

5. 4. 4. 2　Structural model estimate results

The unstandardized and standardized structural model maximum likelihood estimate

(MLE) coefficients of the latent and observed exogenous variables to the latent endogenous variable is presented in tabular and graphically. The empirical result indicated that land fragmentation risk perception, subjective norm and social incentives are positive and significantly predicted the smallholder farmers' adaptive intention towards land fragmentation. Whereas, the smallholder farmers land fragmentation adaptive behavior to their motivation to mitigate land fragmentation is insignificant. Further, the exogenous observed variables such as farmland size and number of plots has a significant effect on smallholder farmers' motivation to land fragmentation mitigation, while land fragmentation index and Shannon crop diversification index are insignificant.

Table 10 Parameter estimation result of structural equation in the level of Smallholder farmers land fragmentation adaptation intentions, Central Highlands of Ethiopia

Parameter	Unstandardized Estimate	Standardized Estimate		S. E.	C. R.	P
		Structural Model				
η5←η1	0.051	0.113	(H1)	0.024	2.123	＊＊
η5←η2	0.372	0.370	(H2)	0.060	6.165	＊＊＊
η5←η3	-0.002	-0.004	(H3)	0.021	-0.079	ns
η5←η4	0.218	0.226	(H4)	0.051	4.309	＊＊＊
η5←K1	-0.065	-0.130	(H5)	0.033	-1.953	＊
η5←K2	0.018	0.118	(H6)	0.010	1.780	＊
η5←K3	-0.017	-0.005	(H7)	0.184	-0.095	ns
η5←K4	0.001	0.001	(H8)	0.053	0.019	ns
		Measurement Model				
X1←η1	1.000	0.884		—	—	—
X2←η1	0.925	0.787		0.047	19.662	＊＊＊
X3←η1	0.932	0.828		0.044	21.416	＊＊＊
X4←η1	0.851	0.806		0.042	20.479	＊＊＊
X5←η1	0.782	0.778		0.041	19.301	＊＊＊
X6←η2	0.793	0.649		0.064	12.427	＊＊＊

Continued Table

Parameter	Unstandardized Estimate	Standardized Estimate	S. E.	C. R.	P
Measurement Model					
X7← η2	1. 000	0. 817	—	—	—
X8← η2	0. 861	0. 716	0. 063	13. 684	* * *
X9← η2	0. 862	0. 717	0. 063	13. 697	* * *
X10←η3	1. 000	0. 843	—	—	—
X11←η3	0. 847	0. 732	0. 053	16. 031	* * *
X12←η3	0. 965	0. 802	0. 053	18. 056	* * *
X13←η3	0. 881	0. 832	0. 047	18. 864	* * *
X14←η4	0. 865	0. 770	0. 044	19. 464	* * *
X15←η4	0. 997	0. 922	0. 040	24. 664	* * *
X16←η4	1. 000	0. 905	—	—	—
Y11←η5	1. 000	0. 744	—	—	—
Y12←η5	0. 929	0. 743	0. 066	14. 037	* * *
Y13←η5	0. 983	0. 759	0. 069	14. 316	* * *
Y14←η5	0. 923	0. 720	0. 068	13. 607	* * *
Y15←η5	0. 927	0. 718	0. 068	13. 568	* * *
Covariance					
η1↔η2	0. 034	0. 103	0. 019	1. 798	*
η1↔η3	0. 15	0. 178	0. 048	3. 151	* * *
η2↔η3	0. 078	0. 203	0. 023	3. 397	* * *
K1↔K2	1. 324	0. 664	0. 119	11. 121	* * *
K1↔K3	− 0. 014	− 0. 158	0. 005	− 3. 145	* * *
K1↔K4	− 0. 056	− 0. 180	0. 016	− 3. 556	* * *
K2↔K3	− 0. 035	− 0. 118	0. 015	− 2. 349	* *
K2↔K4	− 0. 14	− 0. 135	0. 052	− 2. 686	* *
K3↔K4	0. 021	0. 453	0. 003	8. 299	* * *

Note: * * * , * * , * , respectively, by 0. 001, 0. 01, 0. 05 statistical significance level test. [ns] is not significant. H1 – H8 are the hypothesis of the study.

In addition, the measurement model showed that all the latent constructs are positive and significantly explained by their observed variables at $p < 0.001$ significant level. The maximum average standardized regression weight is found social incentives (0. 865) and followed by risk perception (0. 817), adaptation behavior (0. 802) and intention/motivation (0. 737), while the minimum average standardized regression weight is found on subjective norm (0. 725) . The variance among latent and observed exogenous variables are highly significant.

5. 5   Discussion

Land fragmentation risk perception is the subjective judgment of smallholder farmers on the characteristics and severity of land fragmentation risks in their village. In this study the smallholder farmers risk perception is measured by five subjective variables and assessed its impact in their adaptation intentions. As showed in Figure 3 , the standardized regression coefficients of risk perceptions to adaptive intentions is 0. 113 and significant at $P < 0.01$ significant level. The result demonstrated that, smallholder farmers perceived of land fragmentation risks are the more intended towards land fragmentation mitigation. In other word, when smallholder farmers perceived of land fragmentation risks their adaptation intention towards land fragmentation will improve by 11. 3 percent. The result completely support the first (H1) conceptual framework hypothesis of this study. Similar result was found by Chan and Lau (2002), Sharifzadeh et al. (2012) and Dang et al. (2014) that risk perception has a significant antecedent to the farmers' behavioral intentions.

Many scholars confirmed that the impact of social pressure on the individual's decision making significantly influenced the environmental and climate change information adaptation intention Chan and Lau (2002), Sharifzadeh et al. (2012) and Dang et al. (2014). Our result also showed that, when smallholder farmers perceived of social pressure from family, farmers group, extension agents and the community their wishful thinking for land fragmentation adaptation intention significantly influenced with 0. 372 regression weight. The result revealed that, social pressure contributed 37. 2% in the smallholder farmers land fragmentation mitigation decision makings. Thus, the result completely support the second (H2) conceptual framework hypothesis of this study. Compared to other latent variables subjective norm has highly predicted the adaptation intention.

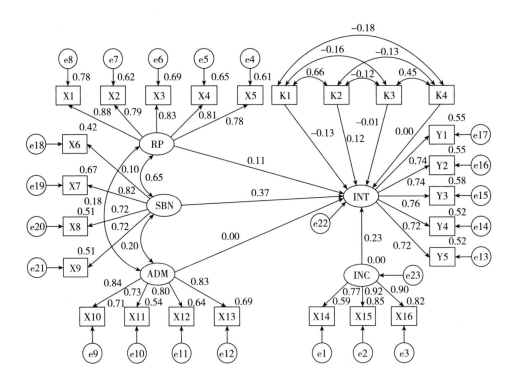

Figure 3　The standardized structural model estimate result of the level of Smallholder farmers adaptation intentions on land fragmentation in the central Highlands of Ethiopia

In many developing countries social infrastructures (incentives) improve the livelihood of the local people and motivated them for resource management and protection as well as better production. In this study we develop a framework to assess the impact of social incentives such as: ①environmental protection program (terracing, plantation) in terms of cash, kind, cost sharing or free; ②access to market and rural bank/credit centers; ③access to extension service centers (agriculture, health, school) on adaptive intentions. The result showed that social incentives significantly enhances the smallholder farmers land fragmentation adaptation intention with 0.226 estimation coefficient and completely support the fourth (H4) conceptual framework hypothesis of this study. The result revealed that, implementing community based participatory watershed management activities, improving access to market and financial centers as well as extension services improves smallholder farmers adaptation intentions by 22.6%. Dong et al. (2014) found that social incentives significantly improve the smallholder farmers climate change adaptation intentions.

Generally, the conceptual framework of this study demonstrated that, when smallholder farmers are perceived of land fragmentation risks, social pressure and social incentives they are: ①the more favorable and the greater likelihood to perform decision making to consolidate their uneconomical, small and spatially dispersed farm parcels; ②the more aspiration moderate to high quality farm parcels and free of land degradation and soil erosion threats/risks; ③the more the anticipation to farm infrastructures such as irrigation and drainage system and road networks; ④the more motivation to use modern agricultural mechanization; ⑤the more inspiration to use recommended farm inputs. However, adaptation behavior/measures ($\eta3$) did not significantly predict the smallholder farmer's adaptive intention levels. In addition, the correlation matrix between adaptation measures and intentions was found weak compared to other predic-

小农户参与可持续土地利用决策比较研究

tors. This might be smallholder farmers are not satisfy with their adaptive behavior and might not perform well. Thus, the result did not support the third (H3) conceptual framework hypothesis of this study.

In addition to the four latent exogenous variables impact on the adaptation intention, in this study we have incorporated four exogenous observed variables in our structural framework such as farmland holding size, number of plots, land fragmentation and crop diversity indexes. The showed that, farmland size (K1) and number of plots (K2) significantly predicts the smallholder farmers' adaptive intention level and completely support the fifth (H5) and sixth (H6) conceptual framework hypothesis of this study. While, the Simpson's land fragmentation index (K3) and Shannon's crop diversity index (K4) are insignificant and which did not support the seventh (H7) and eighth (H8) conceptual framework hypothesis of this study. A negative and significant relationship was found between farmland holding size and adaptive intention with an estimate coefficient of − 0. 130. While a positive and significant causality relationship was found between number of pots and adaptive intentions with 0. 118 regression coefficient. The result demonstrated that farmers having larger farmland holding size their wishful thinking to mitigate land fragmentation was declined by 13 percent. However, farmers having more number of farm parcels their land fragmentation adaptive intention was increased by 11. 8 percent. In addition, farmers who have been practiced crop diversification are more intend to implement land fragmentation mitigation measures. The result revealed that planting different crop species on different farm parcels might not guarantee farmers to maximize crop production and benefited from crop diversification.

In general the estimated coefficients and hypothesis of the constructed conceptual framework model and their expected sign are as expected except H3, H7 and H8. The squared multiple correlations (R^2) are 0. 22 for our land fragmentation adaptive intention conceptual framework. This demonstrated that, a 22 percent variation of farmers land fragmentation adaptive intention in the study areas can be explained by the constructs in our model.

5. 6　Conclusion

Ethiopian agricultural economy is highly dependent on subsistence small – scale farming system. However, the small – scale farming system has been facing many challenges in the sustainable agricultural production of the country, particularly in the Central Highlands of Ethiopia. Land fragmentation is one of the major threats in the study area aside of flooding, drought, climate change, land degradation and soil erosion problems. Taking the advantage of the Theory of Planned Behavior (TPB) and the utility of Structural Equation Modeling (SEM) this study attempted to discover the smallholder farmers' adaptive intention towards land fragmentation. The purpose of this study was twofold: on the one hand to understand the farmers' perspectives and adaptive intention behavior towards land fragmentation mitigation in the Central Highlands of Ethiopia; on the other hand to test the applicability of TPB on land fragmentation adaptive intention through Structural Equation Modeling (SEM) technique. In addition, this study examines land fragmentation status of the study area and its effect on farmers' adaptive intentions. This research might generate some policy implication to authorize an alternative land management program, i. e. , comprehensive land consolidation program in order to improve the agricultural production as well as achieve sustainable rural development in Ethiopia.

Thus, this study concluded that smallholder farmers that more perceived of land fragmentation risks, social pressure, and social infrastructures are: ①the more favorable and the greater likelihood to perform decision making to consolidate their uneconomical, small and spatially dispersed parcels; ②the greater the aspiration of moderate to high quality farm parcels and free of land/soil degradation threats/risks; ③the more the anticipation to farm infrastructures such as irrigation and drainage system and road networks; ④the more motivation to use modern agricultural mechanization; ⑤the more the inspiration to use recommended farm inputs and the more intentions to comprehensive land consolidation in general.

Thus, while the Ethiopian government acknowledges land consolidation on a voluntary basis, this is the right time for Policymakers of the country to plan and implement comprehensive land consolidation in order to improve the agricultural production and achieve sustainable rural development. Constructions of social infrastructures at county (village) level are very useful to improve the adaptive intention level of smallholder farmers towards land fragmentation. Subjective norms are useful tools for dissemination and demonstration of new sustainable land management technologies. However, further study is required in different parts of the country in order to assess the smallholder farmers land fragmentation adaptation intentions to promote and disseminate the efforts of land consolidation.

VI. A Comparative Study on Smallholder Farmers Production Efficiency in China and Ethiopia: The Case of Sichuan Province and the Central Highlands of Ethiopia

6. 1   Introduction

The Chinese and Ethiopian economic growth were poor before their economic reforms and mainly concerned with subsistence agriculture. Since the beginning of economic reforms in 1978 and 1992 in China and Ethiopia, respectively, spectacular fast economic growth has been overlooked and escape hundreds of thousands of people from poverty in both countries. The role of agricultural sector in the building and fostering of the Chinese and Ethiopian economy well known and employed the large labor force. However, in recent years the contribution of agricultural sector to Gross Domestic

Product (GDP) is decreasing while manufacture and service sectors increasing (Gessesse et al. , 2017) .

Many agricultural economists and development specialists agree that smallholder farmers are responsible for a large share of the worlds food production as well as a large share of the food consumption particularly in Africa and Asia countries (FAO, 2012; IFAD and UNEP, 2013; HLPE, 2013; Masters et al. , 2013; Larson et al. , 2014) . The situation in China and Ethiopia smallholder farmers largely involved in the countries grain production. However, the smallholder farmers of China and Ethiopia have faces many challenges such as lack of modern agricultural machinery, fragmented and small farm plots, lack of access of irrigation and drainage system, labor shortage, soil erosion, pests, diseases, drought, and climate change.

Agricultural land is a scares resource due to rapid population growth, land degradation, urbanization and industrial development in China and Ethiopia. The average farm size in China and Ethiopia has decreased in the past three decades. 95% of farms in China are less than 2 hectares and represents 35% of the world's farms (HLPE, 2013) . According to the ERSS (2013) report the average farm size in Ethiopia is 0. 15 ha. In addition, agricultural land fragmentation is one of the challenges that affect the smallholder farmers grain production as well as production efficiency on both countries. To overcome the challenges the Chinese government introduce land consolidation program and investing a large amount of finance and manpower since 1998 and achieved a remarkable result in reclaiming poor soil quality lands, merging uneconomical farm plots and installing modern agricultural infrastructures such irrigation and drainage system and road network. However, comprehensive land consolidation has not yet started in Ethiopia, though the government encourages on a voluntary basis.

Smallholder farmers grain production in China and Ethiopia is one of the major drivers for changes towards sustainable agricultural production with optimal efficiency. Smallholder farmers grain production inefficiency at household level has been identified as major constraints that affect sustainable agricultural production in China and Ethiopia (Chen et al., 2009; Liu and Zhuang, 2000; Geta et al., 2013; Fekadu, 2013; Bachew et al., 2015). However, extensive studies mainly focused on a single crop (mono – cropping system) efficiency performance of smallholder farmers. This might not show the potential efficiency level because crop diversity (multiple – cropping) is common practice of smallholder farmers particularly in the study areas. Furthermore, the earlier studies did not thoroughly investigate the impact of land fragmentation, parcel number, crop diversity, terracing, and land fallowing on smallholder farmers efficiency performance rather than the demographic and social factors.

Thus, the current study undertake a research to fill the information gap and sought the potential determinants of smallholder farmers' production efficiency in Sichuan province and Central Highlands of Ethiopia. The present study employed a Stochastic Frontier Analysis (SFA) and Data Envelopment Analysis for Sichuan province and Central Highlands of Ethiopia, respectively. Therefore, the objective of this study are: ①to estimate the technical efficiency level of Sichuan smallholder farmers where land consolidation program implemented; ②to measure the technical, allocative and economic efficiency of the smallholder farmers in the Central Highlands of Ethiopia under land fragmentation scenario; ③to sort – out the factors affecting the inefficiency of the smallholder farmers in both study area; ④to compare the technical efficiency level between the two study areas. Hence, the findings of this research work might provide information to policymakers, extension and development agents, cooperatives and other social sectors on smallholder farmers crop production efficiency performance and determinants.

6. 2　Research methodology

6. 2. 1　Data

A structured and semi – structured questionnaire was prepared to collect the qualitative and quantitative cross – sectional data. Three districts from Sichuan province and
three woredas of Norther Shewa zone were purposely selected for this study. The three
administrative divisions (namely Neijiang, Ya'an, and Dujiangyan) of Sichuan
province are selected based on their successful implementation of Rural Land Consolidation (RLC) program in partner – based and participatory approach whereas, the three
woredas (namely Debre Birhan, Efratana Gidim and Moretina Jiru) of Northern Shewa
zone were chosen based on their high level of land fragmentation problem. After given
training for data enumerators a face – to – face interview was carried out with 350 and
450 farm household head/spouse of Sichuan province and Central Highlands of Ethiopi-
a, respectively. However, only 186 farm households from Sichuan province and 405
farm households from the Central Highlands of Ethiopia were used for further analysis in
this study.

6. 2. 2　Estimation methods

As we have discussed in Chapter three, there are two most common techniques being used in the measurement of farm efficiency, the parametric or Stochastic Frontier
Approach (SFA) and non – parametric or Data Envelopment Analysis (DEA) (Coel-

li, 1995).

For Sichuan province case study, we have used the Stochastic Frontier Analysis (SFA) which subjected to Cobb – Douglas production function and equation 12 is rewrite as functional form as:

$$y_i = \beta_0 + \sum_{i=1}^{j} \beta_j x_{ij} + (V_i - U_i) \qquad (6-1)$$

Where, y_i is the total grain production output of the ith farm household; x_{ij} is the j types of farm inputs used by the ith farm household; β_0 is the intercept and β_j is the parameters to be estimated.

Basically, we have assumed that the amount of grain output (y_i) of the smallholder farmers varies only due to differences with level of household resource endowment such as farmland size (A), capital (K) and labor (L) and the influences of external factors which are invariables across the farmers such as climate.

Thus, the linear form of Cobb – Douglas stochastic frontier analysis written as:

$$\ln y_i = \beta_0 + \beta_1 \ln A_i + \beta_2 \ln L_i + \beta_3 \ln K_i + (V_i - U_i) \qquad (6-2)$$

The V_i is the random variable which is assumed to be independent and identically distributed (iid) $N(0, \sigma_v^2)$ and the independent of the U_i is non – negative random variable assumed to account for the technical efficiency of production. It's assumed to be independently distributed as truncation at zero of the $N(m_i, \sigma_u^2)$ distribution. Where m_i is technical efficiency level.

Following equation (20), the SFA model parameter estimation is achieved by MLE and the likelihood function estimates indicated in terms of the two variance parameters

$$\gamma = \frac{\sigma_u^2}{\sigma_v^2 + \sigma_u^2}; \ \sigma^2 = (\sigma_v^2 + \sigma_u^2) \qquad (6-3)$$

The Gamma (γ) reflects the validity of the random disturbances (v_i, u_i) proportion of the model and its value between zero and one $(0 \leqslant \gamma \leqslant 1)$. If the value of γ is closer to zero, it means that the variation between actual output and the maximum possible output mainly comes from other uncontrolled pure random factors, which makes the use of the stochastic frontier model is meaningless. In contrast, if the value of γ is closer to one, it indicates that the variation comes mainly from the effects of one or more exogenous (independent) variables that are used in the model.

Whereas, for the Central highlands of Ethiopia case study we have illustrated the Data Envelopment Analysis (DEA) model subjected to input – oriented Variable Return Scale (VRS) due to two reasons: ①smallholder farmers of the study area have more control on farm inputs than farm outputs; ②CRS more preferable when smallholder farmers operate optimal scale but it is impossible as long as smallholder farmers of the study faced input constraints. Thus, to estimate the technical, allocative and economic efficiency we have used 4 input variables such as farm size, seed rate, chemical fertilizer and labor force.

A censored Tobit regression model was used to determine factors affecting the grain production efficiency of the smallholder farmers in both case study area using Maximum Likelihood Estimate.

6. 3   Results

6. 3. 1   Sichuan province case study

6. 3. 1. 1   Stochastic Frontier Analysis result

The Cobb – Douglas stochastic frontier analysis result for Sichuan province is presented in Table 1. The estimates of the variance parameters σ^2 and γ are significantly different at P < 0. 000 significant level. The Gamma (γ) estimation coefficient was 0. 99 which demonstrates that 99% of the variation between the actual and predicted outputs, mainly comes from the variables used in this study. According to Chen et al. (2009) suggestion, the constructed stochastic frontier model Gamma value is satisfactory. Indeed, the MLE results indicated that farmland size, labor and capital are positive and significantly predict the smallholder farmers grain yield output.

Table 1   The stochastic frontier analysis maximum likelihood estimation result

Variable	coefficient	standard – error	t – ratio	P – value
Constant (β_0)	5. 728	0. 165	34. 58	∗∗∗
Farmland size (A)	1. 022	0. 022	46. 42	∗∗∗
Household labor (L)	0. 094	0. 031	3. 041	∗∗∗
Household Capita (K)	0. 008	0. 003	2. 766	∗∗∗
Sigma – squared (σ^2)	0. 208	0. 015	13. 27	∗∗∗
Gamma (γ)	0. 999	0. 000	48768. 8	∗∗∗

Note: ∗∗∗ are statistically significant at P < 0. 0000 significant level.

6. 3. 1. 2 Technical efficiency (TE) result

The TE result was derived from a stochastic frontier estimate at the same time for each sample farmers. As shown in Table 2, the minimum and maximum TE level of the Sichuan smallholder farmers' of grain production is 0. 21 and 1. 00. The minimum technical efficiency score range was found between 0. 21 – 0. 30, while the maximum was between 0. 81 – 0. 90. In addition, 2. 15 percent of the sample smallholder farmers were fully technical efficient. Indeed, more than 51% of the smallholder farmers are above the average TE efficiency of the whole samples.

Table 2   Technical efficiency score of Sichuan farmers' grain production

TE score range	Frequency	Percent	Mean
0. 00 – 0. 10	—	—	—
0. 11 – 0. 20	—	—	—
0. 21 – 0. 30	2	1. 08	0. 21
0. 31 – 0. 40	7	3. 76	0. 37
0. 41 – 0. 50	11	5. 91	0. 47
0. 51 – 0. 60	33	17. 74	0. 56
0. 61 – 0. 70	28	15. 05	0. 67
0. 71 – 0. 80	29	15. 59	0. 75
0. 81 – 0. 90	40	21. 51	0. 85
0. 91 – 1. 00	36	19. 35	0. 69
Total	186	100. 00	0. 73

6. 3. 1. 3   Determinants of technical efficiency of Sichuan province smallholder farmers

The censored Tobit regression model was used to identify the factors affecting the technical efficiency of Sichuan province smallholder farmers' grain production (Table 3). The result showed that the farmland size, irrigation, improved variety, manure and pesticides are positive and significantly enhance the technical efficiency of smallholder producers. However, gender, age, number plots, chemical fertilizer are positive but insignificantly predicted the technical efficiency.

Table 3   Determinants of Sichuan province smallholder farmers

grain production technical efficiency

TE Determinants	Coefficient	Std. Err.	t – statistics	P – value
Sex/gender	0. 007	0. 022	0. 300	0. 763[ns]
Age	0. 000	0. 001	0. 000	0. 998[ns]

TE Determinants	Coefficient	Std. Err.	t − statistics	P − value
Education	0. 016	0. 018	0. 880	0. 379[ns]
Number of plots	0. 015	0. 017	0. 890	0. 374[ns]
Total Farmland holdings	0. 008	0. 003	2. 380	0. 019 **
Access to irrigation	0. 139	0. 026	5. 270	0. 000 ***
Improved variety	0. 077	0. 028	2. 790	0. 006 ***
Chemical fertilizer	0. 027	0. 026	1. 040	0. 300[ns]
Organic fertilizer	0. 159	0. 028	5. 610	0. 000 ***
Pesticide	0. 105	0. 028	3. 790	0. 000 ***
Constant（c）	0. 221	0. 083	2. 650	0. 009 ***
sigma	0. 141	0. 007		
LR chi^2 (10)	88. 23			
Prob > chi^2	0. 0000 ***			
Log likelihood	99. 29			
Pseudo R^2	− 0. 7995			

6. 3. 2　Central Highland of Ethiopia case study

6. 3. 2. 1　Data Envelopment Analysis（DEA）result

The input − oriented VRS technical, allocative and economic efficiencies frequency distribution results of the Central Highlands of Ethiopia are summarized in Table 4. The results noted that the minimum and a maximum TE values were 0. 12 and 1. 0, and the median was 0. 45 which was less than the average TE value of the study area. The result revealed that more than half of the sampled farmers failed to use the minimum feasible amount of inputs to produce a given level of grain yield. The minimum and a maximum AE of smallholder farmers were 0. 03 and 1. 0 values. Whereas the EE were ranged from a minimum of 0. 02 to a maximum of 1. 0.

Table 4　Technical, economic and allocative efficiency of

smallholder grain production

Efficiency Scales	Technical Efficiency (TE)		Economic Efficiency (EE)		Allocative Efficiency (AE)	
	Frequency	%	Frequency	%	Frequency	%
Fully efficient (=1)	29	7.16	1	0.25	1	0.25
0.80 – 0.99	22	5.43	7	1.73	72	17.78
0.60 – 0.79	62	15.31	15	3.70	133	32.84
0.40 – 0.59	127	31.36	68	16.79	139	34.32
0.20 – 0.39	152	37.53	185	45.68	50	12.35
0.00 – 0.19	13	3.21	129	31.85	10	2.47
Mean	0.50		0.30		0.60	
Median	0.45		0.26		0.60	
Minimum	0.12		0.02		0.03	
Maximum	1.00		1.00		1.00	
Std. Error	0.01		0.01		0.01	
Std. Deviation	0.23		0.17		0.19	

6.3.2.2　Input – oriented Isoquants

Isoquant lines are drawn through the set of points at which the same level of output is produced while changing the quantity of the two inputs that show the technology trade – off between the inputs. If input X_1 can be replaced by input X_2 with the same rate to produce a given level of output (Y), the technology trade – off said to be a perfect substitution. However, the technology trade – off described as a perfect complement if and only if input X_1 and X_2 combined efficiently at a certain ratio to maximize the outputs. As shown in Figure 18 (a), (b) and (c), farm size has had perfect complement with seed rate, fertilizer, and labor respectively. In addition, as showed Figure 1 (d) and (e), the seed rate has had perfect complement with fertilizer and labor. The results demonstrated that as the farm size input increased by 1 *timad* (0.25ha) the seed rate, the fertilizer and labor force inputs should increase at least by 38.6kg, 7.1 kg, and 8.4 persons; in addition an increase of 1kg seed input the fertilizer of 0.13kg and 0.2 of labor force should increase to sustain the existing level of smallholder farmers' efficiency in grain production. However, as shown in Figure 1 (f), fertilizer and labor force were perfect substitute inputs. The results disclosed that chemical fertilizer can replace by labor force or vice – verse to maintain the current efficiency level. Therefore, smallholder farmers who are facing a labor shortage can substitute with fertilizer to maintain the existing production efficiency. Additionally, those smallholder farmers facing a shortage of capital to utilize chemical fertilizer require additional labor force to sustain the current efficiency in grain output.

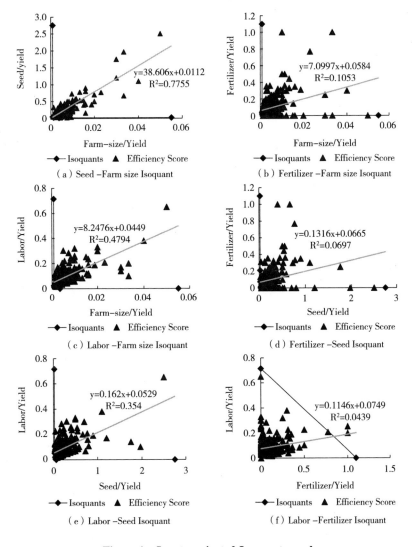

Figure 1　Input – oriented Isoquant graph

6.3.2.3 Factors explaining production inefficiency in the Central Highlands of Ethiopia

The censored Tobit regression model results for factors affecting smallholder farmers' technical, allocative and economic efficiency in grain production of the Central Highlands of Ethiopia are presented in Table 5. The results stated that land fragmentation, crop diversity and parcel numbers were negatively predicted the smallholder farmers' efficiency in grain production. Whereas terracing, manuring, pest management, and land fallowing substantially enhanced the smallholder farmers' efficiency in grain production, in the Central Highlands of Ethiopia.

Table 5 Determinants of technical, allocative and economic

inefficiency of the Central Highlands of Ethiopia

Factors	Technical Efficiency (TE)			Economic Efficiency (EE)			Allocative Efficiency (AE)		
	Coef.	Std. E.	t–value	Coef.	Std. E.	t–value	Coef.	Std. E.	t–value
Land fragmentation	−0.403	0.105	−3.84***	−0.197	0.081	−2.43**	0.061	0.089	0.68^{ns}
Plot number	−0.007	0.007	−1.07^{ns}	0.001	0.005	0.26^{ns}	0.013	0.006	2.21**
Crop diversity	−0.042	0.033	−1.27^{ns}	−0.016	0.026	−0.61^{ns}	0.015	0.028	0.55^{ns}
Terracing	0.078	0.026	2.96***	0.066	0.020	3.24***	0.058	0.022	2.59**
Irrigation system	0.060	0.027	2.25**	0.069	0.021	3.33***	0.046	0.023	2.00**
Manuring	0.012	0.026	0.45^{ns}	0.077	0.020	3.86***	0.126	0.022	5.74***
Pest management	0.045	0.021	2.14**	0.016	0.016	0.98^{ns}	−0.028	0.018	−1.59^{ns}
Land fallowing	0.093	0.026	3.54***	0.051	0.020	2.48**	−0.025	0.022	−1.1^{ns}
_cons	0.721	0.053	13.67***	0.291	0.041	7.15***	0.348	0.045	7.77***
Sigma	0.206	0.007					0.175	0.006	
LRχ^2	73.020			54.050			76.500		
P > χ^2	0.000			0.000			0.000		
R^2	−1.380			−0.193			−0.423		
Log likelihood	62.963			167.037			128.636		

Note: ***, **, * are significant at 1%, 5% and 10% significant level, respectively. ns is non–significant

6. 4 Discussions

For Sichuan province case study, the mean grain production technical efficiency was 0. 73, while the technical, allocative and economic efficiency of the Central Highlands of Ethiopia was 0. 5, 0. 6, and 0. 3, respectively. The result demonstrates that Sichuan province smallholder farmers are technically efficient compared to the Central Highlands of Ethiopia. However, there is still more rooms to further improve the grain production efficiency in both study areas. Chen et al. (2009) and Liu and Zhuang (2000) found an average 0. 68, 0. 55 TE score and higher than that found efficiency among Sichuan province smallholder rice farmers. According to our empirical analysis, smallholder farmers in the Central Highlands of Ethiopia were substantially inefficient in grain production. The considerable part of economic inefficiency was due primarily to technical inefficiency, particularly by poor chemical fertilizer use. Thus, to achieve the maximum EE level the average smallholder farmers could reduce the current actual cost of production by 70% via operating full technical and allocative efficiency. Recent empirical studies conducted by Debebe et al. (2015) and Musa (2011) found 30% and 40% mean EE among smallholder maize farmers in Ethiopia.

Aging, gender (sex), education, number of farm plots and chemical fertilizer are positively enhance the Sichuan farmers' grain production efficiency but are insignificant. The larger landholder farmers were more technically efficient compared to small landholder of farmers. The estimation coefficient of land holding size with respect to TE is 0. 008, which implies that doubling the farm landholding will enhance the TE by

0. 8%. Access to irrigation and drainage system improves the technical efficiency by 0. 14%. Indeed, the utilization of improved variety, organic fertilizer (manure) and pesticides were significantly enhance the TE of grain production by 0. 08%, 0. 16% and 0. 11%, respectively. The result revealed that, there is efficiency gap between agricultural technology users and non – users in Sichuan province. Chen et al. (2003) also found large farm owners were efficient than small farms owners in China.

According to Simpson's index (*SI*) result, the smallholder farmers land fragmentation indexes were range from zero (no fragmentation) to a maximum of 0. 91 (severe fragmentation) with an average of 0. 75 indexes. For farmers who have no land fragmentation the mean TE, EE and AE values were 0. 80, 0. 46, and 0. 56, respectively. Whereas, farmers with moderate land fragmentation indexes ($0. 2 < SI < 0. 5$) the average TE, EE, and AE values were 0. 61, 0. 30, and 0. 51 respectively. Additionally, for farmers having higher land fragmentation indexes ($0. 5 < SI < 0. 7$) the average technical, economic and allocative efficiency values were 0. 51, 0. 30 and 0. 58 respectively. Furthermore, for farmers facing severe land fragmentation ($SI > 0. 7$) were an average technical, economic and allocative efficiency of 0. 46, 0. 29 and 0. 63 respectively. The results demonstrated that smallholder farmers' efficiency in grain production drop with increasing land fragmentation. There was 42. 8% TE and 37. 6% EE gaps found between zero fragmentation and severe fragmentation. In general, as shown in Table 28, land fragmentation has a significant negative effect on smallholder farmers TE and EE with − 0. 383 and − 0. 180 estimation coefficient, respectively. The result demonstrated that land fragmentation seriously affects the smallholder ability to produce maximum grain yield and increases the cost of production in the Central Highlands of Ethiopia. The reason might be due to land fragmentation affects agricultural production system and working condition, increases the transaction cost, and weaken farmers' interest and motivation of investments in land (Tan et al. , 2008; Thomas, 2006; Tashome et al. , 2015) . Hence, land consolidation could be an alternative solution to amalgamate fragmented farm parcels and creation of competitive agricultural production by enabling farmers fewer parcels that are larger and better shaped (Thomas, 2006; Lisec et al. , 2014) .

Some literature found that land fragmentation can be an adaptive strategy and under certain circumstances can have beneficial effects in terms of risk management, crop scheduling, and ecological variety through crop diversification (King and Burton, 1983; Bentley, 1987; Blarel et al. , 1992) . In this study, we sought the effect of crop diversity on smallholder farmers technical, economic and allocative efficiency in grain production. Individual smallholder farmers in the Central Highlands of Ethiopia had an average of three crops and more were sown. According to Shannon's crop diversification index (SHI) , the smallholder farmers crop diversity is range from a minimum of zero (no diversity) to a maximum of 1. 85 with an average of 0. 92 indexes. Farmers who have mono – cropping (no diversity) were more efficient than those who had practice multiple – cropping. The average technical, economic and allocative efficiency values for mono – cropping farmers were 0. 68, 0. 36, and 0. 51 and farmers who had moderately diversified (0. 01 < SHI < 1. 0) were 0. 53, 0. 30, and 0. 59 respectively. Further, for farmers who had higher crop diversity (SHI > 1. 0) their mean TE, EE, and AE values were 0. 44, 0. 28, and 0. 68, respectively. The results revealed that there were 34. 4% of technical and 23. 1% of economic efficiency gaps of mono – cropping (SHI = 0) over multiple – cropping (SHI > 1) . The Tobit regression estimate results also showed that crop diversity negatively predicted the technical and economic efficiency of smallholder farmers with – 0. 05 and – 0. 02 estimation coefficients, respectively. The result demonstrated that farmers the crop diversity by one crop species, their technical and economic efficiency decline by 5% and 2%, respectively. Bachewe et al. (2015) found that households that specialize fully or partially in *Teff* production were more efficient relative to non – specializing households.

Some empirical studies indicated that a higher number of farm plots negatively affect smallholder farmers' grain production as well as efficiency (Thomas, 2006; Tan et al., 2008, Teshome et al., 2015). Our result in the Central Highland of Ethiopia showed that, farmers who have less than five farm parcels had an average technical, economic and allocative efficiency values of 0.52, 0.29 and 0.57 while farmers having six and above farm parcels their mean TE, EE, and AE values were 0.46, 0.30 and 0.65. For farm households having a single farm parcel the mean TE and EE values were 0.77 and 0.44 respectively. The result disclosed that there were 40% technical and 32% economic efficiency gaps farmers having single farm parcel over six and above parcels. In addition, the Tobit regression model results showed that plot number has a negative impact on smallholder TE with an estimated coefficient of −0.003. Whereas, the allocative efficiency of smallholder farmers were positive and statistically significant with 0.02 estimation coefficient. The result revealed that as the number of parcels increases by one the TE dropped by 0.3%, while the EE and AE raised by 0.5% and 1.5%, respectively. The result is consistent with Sichuan province case study and Wang et al. (1996), who demonstrated a positive and significant coefficient of the parcel number on profit efficiency in rice production in China.

Sustainable land management (terracing) is common practices in the Central Highlands of Ethiopia, which implemented to tackle top soil erosion problems and sustain agricultural production while the adoption and quality of SLM technologies are inadequate (Kassie et al., 2009). According to our survey result, 80% of the respondents have implemented land management structures (terracing) whereas the remaining

20% did not. The average TE, EE, and AE values for farmers who implemented terracing were 0.51, 0.31, and 0.62 whereas, 0.46, 0.24, and 0.52 for non – terraced. The results revealed that, there was 9.1% technical, 21.6% economic, and 15.1% allocative efficiency gaps of terraced land over unterraced. The result revealed that sustainable land management plays a crucial role in the improvement of farmers' grain production efficiency. Now, terracing has a positive and significant effect on smallholder farmers' production efficiency. On the other hand, 19.3% farm households had only access to the irrigation system and their mean TE, EC, and AE values were 0.54, 0.36 and 0.66, whereas for non – irrigation was 0.49, 0.28 and 0.58, respectively. The result demonstrated that there were 9.4% technical, 22.2% economic, and 12.1% allocative efficiency gaps of irrigation accessed farmers over non – accessed counterparts. The Tobit regression model also showed that irrigation has a significant positive impact on smallholder farmers' production efficiency. The result is similar with Sichuan province case of this study.

Land fallowing is a practice where farm parcels are unseeded (uncultivated) for seasons. In the Central Highlands of Ethiopia smallholder farmers are widely practiced land fallowing due to: lack of labor and capital resources, distant farm plots from the homestead, and poor soil structure and quality. According to our survey result, more than 28% farm households were unseeded their farmland at least 0.5 *timad* (0.125 ha) during the study period. The average TE, EE, and AE values for farmers practiced land fallowing were 0.52, 0.31, and 0.60 whereas, 0.49, 0.29 and 0.60 for farmers cultivated all their farm plots. We also found that there were 6.6% TE and 8.4% EE gaps of farmers partially seeded over fully seeded counterparts. The Tobit regression model result showed that land fallowing has a significant positive impact on the technical and economic efficiency of smallholder farmers. The result demonstrated that land fallowing is an alternative land use practice to maximize the production efficiency of smallholder farmers. Thus, farmers having more farm plots, but lack of labor and capital acquired land fallowing or share/rent out land to others in order to be technically as well as economically efficient.

Organic fertilizer enhances the water holding capacity, structure and nutrient cycle of the soil as well as improve crop production (Kassie et al., 2009). We examine the effect of manuring on smallholder farmers' grain production efficiency in the Central Highlands of Ethiopia. The result indicated that manuring significantly enhances the smallholder farmers' production efficiency. Mean technical, economic and allocative efficiency values for farmers who had used manuring were 0.50, 0.31 and 0.63 which is higher and statistically significant relative to unused counterparts (0.49, 0.23 and 0.49). We also found that, there was 2.1% technical, 26.6% economic, and 22.7% allocative efficiency gaps of manure users over unused counterparts. Additionally, pest management significantly improves the smallholder farmers' technical efficiency. Mean TE, EE, and AE values for farmers who applied pesticides was 0.51, 0.30, and 0.59, which is higher than unused counterparts (0.49, 0.29 and 0.61). The result demonstrated that pest management importantly contributes to enhance the of smallholder farmers' production efficiency in the Central Highlands of Ethiopia.

6.5　Conclusion

We found that farmland size, labor and capital positive and significantly predict the grain yield output of Sichuan province smallholder farmers. The average technical efficiency of the smallholder grain production was 73% in Sichuan province whereas the technical allocative and economic efficiency of the Central Highlands of Ethiopia was 50% , 60% and 30% , respectively. The result confirms that Sichuan farmers are technically efficient compared to the Central Highlands of Ethiopia. Therefore, there is further need to improve the grain production efficiency in both study areas particularly in the Central Highlands of Ethiopia. In addition, landholding size, irrigation, improved variety, manure and pesticides are positive and significantly enhance the technical efficiency of Sichuan province smallholder producers whereas, gender, age, number plots, chemical fertilizer are insignificant. Indeed, land fragmentation, crop diversity and parcel numbers are negatively predicted the smallholder farmers' efficiency in grain production the Central Highlands of Ethiopia whereas terracing, manuring, pest management, and land fallowing substantially enhanced the smallholder farmers' efficiency.

Therefore, demonstration of agricultural technologies (inputs) at household level and reducing land fragmentation though comprehensive land consolidation program is crucial in order to improve the grain production as well as efficiency of smallholder farmers in Sichuan and in the Central Highlands of Ethiopia.

VII. General Conclusion and Policy Implications

7. 1 Conclusions

Before the opening – up of economic reform, the agricultural economic development in China and Ethiopia was unfortunate and conquered by small – scale subsistence farming system. However, with the onset of economic reforms in 1978 in China and in 1992 in Ethiopia, the virtual share of the agricultural economy in the country's gross domestic product (GDP) substantially raise year on year. Hence, spectacular fast economic growth has been overlooked with approximate 10 percent annual GDP increment in the past decades and escapes hundreds of thousands of people from poverty in both countries. However, there is still food insecurity at household level which remain as an issue in many rural areas of both countries particularly in Ethiopia. Agricultural land in many rural areas of China and Ethiopia is profound as people's living standard, wealth, social status and aspirations indicator that transferred across generations. Thus, proper utilization, governing and administrating of agricultural lands therefore has a significant impact on the countries future economic growth. However, agricultural land is a scare resource in China and Ethiopia due to the conversion to urban and industrial developments, rapid population growth, and bio – physical as well as institutional related issues. Indeed, existence of land fragmentation in China and Ethiopia is one of the major obstacle for modern agricultural mechanization and irrigation and drainage systems that affect production efficiency as well as sustainable grain production. Hence, the share of agriculture in the economic growth declining year on year in China and Ethiopia. To overcome the challenges of agricultural production and achieve sustainable rural development, China has investing a large amount of manpower, material and financial resources in comprehensive land consolidation programs and achieving a remarkable result in reclaiming poor quality soils into medium and high quality, merging small and fragmented parcels change to larger and better shape, installing agricultural infrastructures such as irrigation and drainage systems, road network in many project areas, especially Sichuan province. While in Ethiopia, the comprehensive land consolidation is not yet start. The current PhD thesis is intended to provide the information gaps on the perspectives and adaptive intention of smallholder farmers on land consolidation and fragmentation for optimal production efficiency in China and Ethiopia, particularly in Sichuan province and the Central Highlands of Ethiopia. Therefore, the objective of this PhD thesis are: ①to understand the Sichuan smallholder farmers' awareness, perception and adaptation intention of land consolidation and rehabilitation; ②to explore the local farmers perspective and adaptation intention behavior towards land fragmentation in the Central Highlands of Ethiopia; ③to assess, examine and compare the smallholder farmers production efficiency and its determinants in Sichuan province and the Central

Highlands of Ethiopia. The findings of this thesis might help policymakers, development agents, agricultural sectors, researchers and academicians working on sustainable to assess the local farmers' awareness, perception and adaptation intentions towards land consolidation and fragmentation.

The current PhD thesis work is carried out in Sichuan province, China and Amhara region, Ethiopia. Sichuan province is located in the upper reaches of the Yangtze River Valley in the Southwest of China. Rice (*Oryza sativa*), wheat (*Tritcum*), maize (*Zea mays*) and sweet potato (*Ipomoea batatas*) are the major staple food crops and peanut (*Arachis hypogaea*), cotton (*Gossypium arboretum*), tobacco (*Nicotiana*) and tea (*Camellia sinensis*) are the most cash (economic) crops in Sichuan province. Amhara region is one of the nine ethnic divisions located in the north western and north central part of Ethiopia. Teff (*Eragrostis tef*), barley (*Hordeum vulgare*), wheat (*Triticum*), sorghum (*Sorghum bicolor*) and maize (*Zea mays*) are the major crops and cotton (*Gossypium hirsutum*), sesame (*Sesamum indicum*), sunflower (*Helianthus annuus*), and sugarcane (*Saccharum officinarum*) are the main cash crops. This academic research was carried out in three purposely selected districts from each study province/region. Neijiang, Dujiangyan and Ya'an districts from Sichuan province and Debre Birhan, Efratana Gidim and Moretina Jiru districts from Amhara region choose based on their successful participators land consolidation program and high rate of land fragmentation level, respectively. This enables the researcher to identify the smallholder farmers' adaptation decisions to land fragmentation and consolidation for optimal production efficiency of the study areas. Thus, farm household questionnaires were prepared to collect qualitative and quantitative primary data, which the original English version questionnaires translated into Simplified Chinese and Amharic version for Sichuan and Amhara region, respectively. A simple random sampling technique was used to carry out a face –

to – face interview with 350 smallholder farmers from Sichuan province and 450 smallholder farmers from Amhara region. However, 331 and 405 samples were valid and used for further analysis in this PhD thesis from Sichuan province and Amhara region, respectively. The overall sample households demographic characteristics from both study areas are good representation to ensure the reliability and validity of the questionnaire. Therefore, the sample farm household data were used for empirical analysis to test the hypothesis and to verify the theoretical model of this study. Thus, to achieve the objectives and hypothesis of this PhD study four econometric models were employed. The Structural Equation Modeling (SEM) was used to understand the perspective and adaptive intention of smallholder farmers' to land fragmentation and consolidation. Whereas, the Stochastic Frontier Analysis (SFA) and Data Envelopment Analysis (DEA) were utilized to estimate the smallholder farmers grain production efficiency. Indeed, Tobit regression model was employed to investigate the factors affecting the smallholder farmers' grain production inefficiency. IBM – AMOS 22. 0, IBM – SPSS 22. 0, Frontier 4. 1, max DEA 7. 0 and STATA 14. 0 statistical software were also utilized in this study.

Thus, prior to CFA – SEM model estimation, the collected structural data adequacy, internal consistency reliability and validity was checked using Cronbach's alpha, KMO, factor loadings, AVE, CR, and SQR – AVE. Therefore, the result showed that the collected data from both study areas are adequate, internally consistent, reliable and valid to proceed factor analysis. Then, we determined the measurement model and structural model factor analysis using CFA and checked by Goodness – of – Fit (GOF) indexes such as Chi – square indexes (CMIN, degree of freedom and CMIN/df), absolute fit indexes (GFI, RMSEA, RMR, and SRMR), incremental NFI, TLI, CFI and RNI), and the parsimony fit indexes (AGFI, P – CLOSE, and PNFI). Thus, according to the model fit criterion, we found the overall land fragmentation and land consolidation conceptual frameworks goodness – of – fit are at acceptable ranges and no model modification was carried out in both case studies.

The land consolidation adaptive intention theoretical model of Sichuan province case study has consists of eight testable hypothesis: (H1) media has a positive and significant impact on the development of farmers' awareness towards land consolidation; (H2) media has a positive and significant impact on the development of farmers' perception to land consolidation and rehabilitation programs implementing in their village; (H3) media contribute a positive and significant role to perform farmers' land consolidation adaptation intention decisions; (H4) social network has a positive and significant impact on the development of farmers' awareness towards land consolidation; (H5) Social network has a positive significant impact on the development of farmers' perception to land consolidation and rehabilitation programs implementing in their village; (H6) social network contribute a positive and significant effect to perform farmers' land consolidation adaptation intention decisions; (H7) farmers the more aware of land consolidation are the more intended to perform land consolidation adaptation decisions finally; (H8) farmers the more perceived of land consolidation and rehabilitation program implementing in their village are the more intended to perform land consolidation adaptation decisions. There are five latent such as Media. Social network, Awareness, Perception and Adaptation intention variables and twenty five observed (measured) variables were used in the land consolidation adaptation model. The standardized structural model confirms that Media and Social – network significantly enhance the perception and awareness of smallholder farmers towards land consolidation. In addition, social – network, awareness, and perception significantly predict the smallholder farmers land consolidation adaptation intention decisions. The effect of Social network to perform farmers' land consolidation adaptation intention decisions is 44 percent whereas

Media is 5. 3 percent. The short communication materials (flyers, brochures and leaf-lets) are play key role in the development of farmers' awareness, perception, and ad-aptation intention decisions and followed by Electronic (Radio and Television) broad-cast, local Newspapers and the Internet. When farmers are aware and perceived of land consolidation and rehabilitation program implemented in their village their adaptation in-tention decisions to use agricultural inputs such as fertilizer, improved seed, and ma-chinery significantly improved by 21 and 14 percent, respectively. The standardized structural model findings confirms that Social network plays a significant role in the de-velopment of farmers' awareness, perception as well as adaptation intentions of land consolidation. Hence, our results conclude that Social network is a useful tool to dissem-ination, demonstration, and promotion the efforts of land consolidation and rehabilita-tion program as well as to improve the individual and collective awareness, perception and adaptation intention decision – making than Media.

Land fragmentation is one of the major agricultural production obstacle of small-holder farmers in Ethiopia, particularly in the Central Highlands of Ethiopia. Studies on farmers' attitude, perceptions and adaptive intentions towards land fragmentation are limited particularly in Ethiopia. Some scholars used descriptive statistics and Analysis of Variance (ANOVA) to understand farmers' perception on sustainable land manage-ment in Ethiopia. However, these models did not indicate the net influence of factors on the response variable and did not distinguish the causal pathways that link cause and effect of the variables. The present study is based on plausible methodological similarities with behavior and psychological studies and adopting of the Theory of Planned Behavior (TPB) and utility of Structural Equation Model (SEM) techniques to fill the gap in the causality relationship as well as the direct and indirect effect of land fragmentation risk perception, adaptation measure, subjective norm and social incentives on farmers' land fragmentation mitigation intentions. Thus, understanding the private adaptive intention behavior towards land fragmentation in the Ethiopia, particularly in the Central Highlands of Ethiopia is very crucial for Policymakers to plan and implement alternative comprehensive land management tools such as land consolidation to improve the agricultural production as well as sustainable rural development in the country. This study has answered the following research questions: ①to what extent the farmers' perspectives on land fragmentation risk perception affect their adaptive intention level; ②to what extent the farmers' adaptation behavior/measures affect their land fragmentation mitigation intention level; ③does the social pressure and social incentive affect the farmers land fragmentation mitigation intention. To test the research hypotheses and to synthesize the conceptual framework of the study, five latent variables and twenty five observed (measured) variables have been used. The standardized structural model result indicated that when smallholder farmers perceived of land fragmentation risks their adaptation intention towards land fragmentation improve by 11.3%. In addition, when smallholder farmers perceived of social pressure from family, farmers group, extension agents and the community their wishful thinking of land fragmentation mitigation decision makings significantly enhanced by 37.2%. Further, social incentives such as environmental protection program (terracing, plantation) in terms of cash, kind, cost sharing or free, access to market and rural bank/credit centers, and access to extension service centers (agriculture, health, school) significantly enhance the smallholder farmers land fragmentation adaptation intention by 22.6%. Our result conclude that, when smallholder farmers are perceived of land fragmentation risks, social pressure and social incentives they are: ①the more favorable and the greater likelihood to perform decision making to land consolidation; ②the more aspiration moderate to high quality farm parcels and free of land degradation and soil erosion threats/risks; ③the more the anticipation to farm infrastructures; ④the more motivation to use modern agricultural mechanization; ⑤The more inspiration to use recommended farm inputs. Indeed, smallholder farmers having large farm size, more farm parcels, less crop diversity, and higher land fragmentation problems are highly intended to land consolidation.

In the Chapter six of this PhD thesis, we try to investigate the smallholder farmers grain production efficiency in Sichuan province and in the Central Highlands of Ethiopia with the application of Stochastic Frontier Analysis (SFA) and Data Envelopment Analysis (DEA). The maximum likelihood estimate result indicated that farmland size, labor and capital are positive and significantly predict the grain yield output of Sichuan province. In addition, smallholder farmers in Sichuan province are 73% technical efficient in grain production. While the Central Highlands of Ethiopia smallholder farmers are 50% technical, 60% allocative and 30% economic efficient. Sichuan province smallholder farmers are more technically efficient compared to the Central Highlands of Ethiopia, but there is still more rooms to further improve the efficiency in both study areas. Farmland size, irrigation, improved variety, manure and pesticides are positive and significantly enhance the technical efficiency of Sichuan smallholder farmers. In the Central Highlands of Ethiopia land fragmentation, crop diversity and parcel numbers negatively predict the smallholder farmers' efficiency whereas terracing, manuring, pest management, and land fallowing substantially enhance the efficiency.

7.2　Policy implications

Since 1998 China has spending billions of yuan in land consolidation program and significantly reclaiming degraded lands, reducing land fragmentation, improving of agricultural infrastructures, and building clean and tidy villages, particularly in many rural areas of Sichuan province. However, in order to authorize and promote the efforts of land consolidation and rehabilitation program in Sichuan province understandings the local farmers' awareness and perception of land consolidation is very crucial. In this regard, the contribution of electronic and printing media are insignificant. Thus, the local government authority is much more expected to use Media particularly the local Newspapers and the Internet to authorize and promote the efforts of land consolidation and rehabilitation program in rural areas of Sichuan province as well as to improve the local farmers' awareness, perception, and adaptation intention in order to improve the agricultural production efficiency and achieve sustainable rural development.

Land fragmentation is one of the major threats of Ethiopian agricultural economy aside of flooding, drought, climate change, land degradation and soil erosion problems. Understanding the perspective and adaptive intention of the local farmers towards land fragmentation is very crucial to policymakers to plan and implement a comprehensive land management tools such as land consolidation. However, comprehensive land consolidation is not started yet in Ethiopian. Therefore, now this is the right time for policymakers of the country to plan and implement comprehensive land consolidation in order to improve the agricultural production efficiency and achieve sustainable rural development.

References

[1] Action Aid Ethiopia. Policies and Practices for Securing and Improving Access to and Control over Land in Ethiopia. Paper presented at FAO International Conference on Agrarian Reform and Rural Development held in Porto Alegre, Brazil, 2006 (3): 7 – 10. http://www. fig. net/resources/proceedings/fig_ proceedings/fig2006/papers/ts71/ts71_ 01_ cotula_ etal_ 0879. pdf.

[2] Benjamin, D. and Brandt L. . Property rights, labor markets, and efficiency in a transition economy: the case of rural China. Canadian Journal of Economics, 2002, 35 (4): 689 – 716.

[3] Bentley, J. W. . Economic and Ecological Approaches to Land Fragmentation: In Defense of a Much – Maligned Phenomenon. *Annual Review of Anthropology*, 1987, 16: 31 – 67.

[4] Berndt, E. R. and L. R. Christensen. . The Translog Function and the Substitution of Equipment, Structures, and Labor in U. S. Manufacturing 1929 – 1968. *Journal of Econometrics*, 1973, 1 (1): 81 – 113.

[5] Binswanger, H. P. . A Cost Function Approach to the Measurement of Elasticities of Factor Demand and Elasticities of Substitution. *American Journal of Agricultural*

Economics, 1974, 56 (2): 377 – 386.

[6] Blarel B, Hazell P, Place F, Quiggin J. . The economics of farm fragmentation: evidence from Ghana and Rwanda. World Bank Economic Review, 1992, 6 (2): 233 – 54.

[7] Di Falco, S. , Penov, I. , Aleksiev, A. and Van Rensburg, T. M. . Agrobiodiversity, farm profits and land fragmentation: Evidence from Bulgaria. *Land Use Policy*, 2010, 27: 763 – 771.

[8] Bramall, C. . Chinese Land Reform in Long – Run Perspective and in the Wider East Asian Context. Journal of Agrarian Change, 2004, 4 (1): 101 – 141.

[9] Bruce, J, Wendland, K. , and Naughton T. L. . Whom to pay? Key Concepts and Terms regarding Tenure and Property Rights in Payment – based Forest Ecosystem Conservation. Madison, WI: Land Tenure Center, 2010.

[10] Bruce, John W. Hobben, Allan, Desalegn Rahmato. After the Derg an Assessment of Rural Land Tenure Issues in Ethiopia. (Unpublished, A Collaborative Project of Land Tenure Centre, University of Wiscosin Medison and The Institute of Development Research, Addis Ababa University), p. 107 http: //minds. wisconsin. edu/ handle/1793/61013, 1994.

[11] Chakraborty, S. , Banik, D. . Design of a material handling equipment selection model using analytic hierarchy process. The International Journal of Advanced Manufacturing Technology, 2006, 28: 1237 – 1245.

[12] Chen, F. , and Davis, J. . Land Reform in Rural China since the mid – 1980s. Land Reform, Land Settlement, and Cooperatives (FAO), 1998, 6 (2): 123 – 137.

[13] Chen, J. . On property institution of the People's Commune. Economic Research, 1994, 7: 47 – 53.

[14] Chuttur, M. Y.. Overview of the technology acceptance model: Origins, developments and future directions. Working Papers on Information Systems, 2009, 9 (37): 9 – 37.

[15] Demetris Demetrious. The Development of an Integrated Planning and Decision Support System (IPDSS) for Land Consolidation. Springer PhD Thesis, 2014.

[16] Dessalegn Rahmato. Revisiting the Land Issue: Options for Change. Economic Focus, 1999, 2 (4): 9 – 11.

[17] EEA (Ethiopian Economic Association). Research report on land tenure and agricultural development in Ethiopia. Ethiopian Economics Association: Addis Ababa, 2002.

[18] Ellis, F.. Peasant economics. Farm Household in Agrarian Development. Cambridge University Press, London, 1992.

[19] Ellis G. M. , Fisher A. C. Valuing the environment as input. J Environ Manag, 1987, 25: 149 – 156.

[20] FAO. The design of land consolidation pilot projects in Central and Eastern Europe. Rome: FAO, 2003.

[21] FAO. Land Tenure Studies: Land Tenure and Rural Development. Land Tenure Studies Series. Land Tenure Service of the Rural Development Division, 2002.

[22] FAO. Strategy for land consolidation and improved land management in Armenia. Pre – feasibility study by K. Chluba; E. Schmidt – Kallert. FAO Subregional Office, Budapest, 2001.

[23] FDRE (Federal Democratic Republic of Ethiopia). Constitution of the Federal Democratic Republic Of Ethiopia. Addis Ababa. http: //www. moa. gov. et/ web/pages/proclamationland, 1995.

[24] FDRE (Federal Democratic Republic of Ethiopia). Proclamation No. 456/

2005. Federal Democratic Republic of Ethiopia Rural Land Administration and Use Proc-lamation, Addis Ababa, 2005.

[25] FDRE (Federal Democratic Republic of Ethiopia). Proclamation No. 455/ 2005. A Proclamation to Provide for the Expropriation of Landholdings for Public purpo-ses and Payment of Compensation, Addis Ababa, 2005.

[26] FDRE (Federal Democratic Republic of Ethiopia). Proclamation No. 89/ 1997. Rural Land Administration Proclamation, 1997.

[27] Fei, X.. Peasant Life in China: A Field Study of Country Life in the Yan-gtze Valley. E. P. Dutton, New York, 1939.

[28] Garrod G. , Willis K. G.. Economic valuation of the environment. Edward Elgar Publishing Ltd. , Cheltenham, 1999.

[29] Haile, M. , Witten, W. , Abraha, K. , Fissha, S. , Kebede, A. , Kassa, G. and Reda, G.. Research Report 2. Land Registration in Tigray, Northern E-thiopia, 2005.

[30] He, C. , Huang, Z. and Wang, W.. Land use changes and economic growth in China. Land Lines, 2012: 14 - 19.

[31] He Ge. Farmland Acquisition System in China: Problems and Respon-ses. Canadian Social Science, 2012, 8 (4): 258 - 263.

[32] Ho, Peter. Developmental Dilemmas: Land Reform and Institutional Change in China. Routledge, New York, USA, 2005.

[33] Holden, S. , Shiferaw, B. and Pender, J.. Market Imperfections and Land Productivity in the Ethiopian Highlands. *Journal of Agricultural Economics*, 2001, 52: 53 - 70.

[34] Hristov, J.. Assessment of the impact of high fragmented land upon the pro-ductivity and profitability of the farms: the case of the Macedonian vegetable grow-

ers. Faculty of Natural Resources and Agricultural Sciences, 2009.

[35] Huang, Q. H. , Li, M. C. , Chen, Z. J. , and Li, F. X.. Land consolidation: an approach for sustainable development in rural China. AMBIO, 2011, 39 (1): 93 –95.

[36] Hung, V. , Pham, Macaulay, P. , T. Gordon and Marsh, S. P.. The economics of land fragmentation in the north of Vietnam. *Australian Journal of Agricultural and Resource Economics*, 2007, 51: 195 –211.

[37] Igozurike, M. U.. Land tenure, social relations and the analysis of spatial discontinuity. Area, 1974, 6: 132 –135.

[38] Jabarin, A. S. , and Epplin, F. M.. Impacts of land fragmentation on the cost of producing wheat in the rain – fed region of northern Jordan. Agricultural Economics, 1994, 11 (2 –3): 191 –196.

[39] Januszewski, J.. Index of land consolidation as a criterion of the degree of concentration. Geographia Polonica, 1968, 14: 291 –296.

[40] King, R. , and Burton, S.. Structural change in agriculture: the geography of land consolidation. Progress in Human Geography, 1982, 7 (4): 471 –501.

[41] Kurttila, M. , Pesonen, M. , Kangas, J. , Kajanus, M.. Utilizing the analytic hierarchy process (AHP) in SWOT analysis – a hybrid method and its application to a forest – certification case. Forest Policy and Economics, 2000, 1 (1): 41 –52.

[42] Li, Jian. A literature review on reform of the Chinese land tenure system. References for studies on rural economy. Beijing Ministry of Agriculture, 1995.

[43] Li Ling and David Isaac. The Development of Urban Land Policy in China. Property Management, 1994, 12 (4): 12 –17.

[44] Li Yurui, Liu Yansui, Long Hualou, and Cui Weiguo. Community – based

rural residential land consolidation and allocation can help to revitalize hollowed villages in traditional agricultural areas of China: Evidence from Dancheng County, Henan Province Yurui. Land Use Policy, Elsevier. inc, 2014, 39: 188 – 198.

[45] Liu, Y. S., Yang, R., Li, Y. H.. Potential of land consolidation of hollowed villages under different urbanization scenarios in China. Journal of Geographical Sciences, 2013, 23 (3): 503 – 512.

[46] Liu, S., Carter, M. R. and Yao, Y.. Dimensions and diversity of property rights in rural China: Dilemmas on the road to further reform. World Development, 1998, 26 (10): 1789 – 1806.

[47] Mc Pherson, M.. Land fragmentation: a selected literature review *Development Discussion Paper*, 1982: 141.

[48] Melkamu B. and Shewakena A.. Facing the challenges in building Sustainable Land Administration Capacity in Ethiopia, (FIG Congress, Facing the Challenges – Building the Capacity Sydney, Australia, 2010 (4): 11 – 16.

[49] Nega, Berhanu, Berhanu Adenew, and Samuel Gebre Sellasie. "Current land policy issues in Ethiopia." Land Reform, Land Settlement, and Cooperatives, 2003: 103 – 124.

[50] Nguyen, T., Cheng, E., and Findlay, C.. Land fragmentation and farm productivity in China in the 1990. China Economic Review, 1996, 7 (2): 169 – 180.

[51] Niroula, G. S. and Thapa, G. B.. Impacts and causes of land fragmentation, and lessons learned from land consolidation in South Asia. *Land Use Policy*, 2005, 22: 358 – 372.

[52] Ping Li. Rural land tenure reforms in China: Issues, regulations and prospects for additional reform. Land Reform, Land Settlement and Cooperatives, 2003

(3): 59 – 72.

[53] Ram, K. A., Tsunekawa, A., Sahad, D. K., and Miyazaki, T.. Subdivision and fragmentation of land holdings and their implication in desertification in the Thar Desert, India. Journal of Arid Environments, 1999, 41 (4): 463 – 477.

[54] Saaty, T. L.. The Analytic Hierarchy Process. McGraw – Hill, New York, 1980.

[55] Segers, K., Dessein, J., Hagberg, S., Teklebirhan, Y., Haile, M. and Deckers, J.. Unravelling the dynamics of access to farmland in Tigray, Ethiopia: The emerging land market? revisited. *Land Use Policy*, 2010, 27: 1018 – 1026.

[56] Shimelles Tenaw, K. M. Zahidul Islam and Tuulikki Parviainen. Effects of land tenure and property rights on agricultural productivity in Ethiopia, Namibia and Bangladesh, University of Helsinki Department of Economics and Management Discussion Papers No. 33, Helsinki. http: //www. helsinki. fi/taloustiede/Abs/DP33. pdf, 2009.

[57] Simion, G.. Geographical analysis of the land fragmentation process based on participatory mapping and satellite images. Case studies of Ciorogarla and Vanatorii Mici from the Bucharest metropolitan area. Human Geographies 2 – 1. Bucharest, 2008.

[58] Simmons, A. J.. An index of farm structure, with a Nottinghamshire example. East Midlands Geographer, 1964, 3: 255 – 261.

[59] Stavis, B.. Rural institutions in China. In R. Barker, R. Sinha and B. Rose, eds. The Chinese agricultural economy. Boulder, Colorado, USA, Westview Press/London, UK, Croom Helm, 1982.

[60] Tan, S., H., N., Kruseman, G. and Qu, F.. Do fragmented landholdings have higher production costs? Evidence from rice farmers in Northeastern Jiangxi province, P. R. China. *China Economic Review*, 2008, 19: 347 – 358.

［61］ Tan, S. H. , Heerink, N. , and Qu, F. T. . Land fragmentation and its driving forces in China. Land Use Policy, 2006, 23: 272 – 285.

［62］ Tan S. . Land fragmentation and rice production: a case study small farms in Jiangxi province, china. PhD Thesis Washington University, 2005.

［63］ Thomas Joachim. What's on Regarding Land Consolidation in Europe? Shaping the Change. XXIII FIG Congress, Munich, Germany, 2006: 8 – 13.

［64］ Thomas Joachim. Property Rights, Land Fragmentation and Emerging Structure of Agriculture in Central and East European Countries. Food and Agriculture Organization – CUREMIS II, Rome, 2005.

［65］ Thomas, J. . Property rights, land fragmentation and the emerging structure of agriculture in Central and Eastern European countries. Food and Agriculture Organization, Rome, 2004.

［66］ Tobin, James. "Estimation of relationships for limited dependent variables". Econometrica. doi: 10. 2307/1907382. JSTOR 1907382, 1958, 26 （1）: 24 – 36.

［67］ USAID （United States of America International Development）. Ethiopia Land Policy and Administration Assessment. USAID Contract No. LAG – 00 – 98 – 00031 – 00, Task Order No. 4. http: //pdf. usaid. gov/pdf _ docs/Pnacx751. pdf, 2004.

［68］ Vaidya, O. S. , Kumar, S. . Analytic hierarchy process: an overview of applications. European Journal of Operational Research, 2006, 169 （1）: 1 – 29.

［69］ Van Dijk, T. . Effects of land consolidation in practice analysis of post – war experience in the Netherlands. In E. M. Fendel （Ed. ）, Proceedings of 22nd urban and regional data management symposium Seminar on land markets and land consolidation in Central Europe. Delft: TU Delft, 2000.

[70] Vitikainen, A.. An overview of land consolidation in Europe. Nordic Journal of Surveying and Real Estate Research, 2004, 1: 25 – 43.

[71] Vladan Dokic, Stevan Marosan. New Model of Land Consolidation and Rural Development in Serbia, 2008.

[72] Wan, G. H. and Cheng, E.. Effects of land fragmentation and returns to scale in the Chinese farming sector. *Applied Economics*, 2001, 33: 183 – 194.

[73] Wang, Q. , Zhang, M. , and Cheong, K.. Stakeholder perspectives of China's land consolidation program: a case study of Dongnan Village, Shandong Province. M Habitat International, 2014, 43: 172 – 180.

[74] Wang, S. Y.. Review of land consolidation at home and abroad. Beijing: China Land Press, 1997.

[75] Wu, Z. P. , Liu, M. Q. , Davis, J.. Land consolidation and productivity in Chinese household crop production. China Economic Review, 2005, 16: 28 – 49.

[76] Wu, H. X.. Reform in China's Agriculture, Briefing Paper Series, 9, Department of Trade, Australia, 1997.

[77] Xie GD, Lu CX, Leng YF, Zheng D. Ecological assets valuation of the Tibetan Plateau. Journal of Natural Resources, 2003, 18: 189 – 196.

[78] Yan, J.. China's land use and planning research strategy. Beijing: China Land Press (in Chinese), 2010.

[79] Yang, X.. Land Privatization and Constitutional Rule, Collections of Yang Xiaokai, 2003.

[80] Yirsaw, E. , Wu, W. , Shi, X. , Temesgen, H. and Bekele, B.. Land Use/Land Cover Change Modeling and the Prediction of Subsequent Changes in Ecosystem Service Values in a Coastal Area of China, the Su – Xi – Chang Region. Sustainability, 2017, 9 (7): 1204.

［81］ FAO. The State of Food and Agriculture 2012: Investing in agriculture for a better future. Rome: FAO, 2012.

［82］ IFAD & UNEP. Smallholders, food security and the environment. Rome, 2013.

［83］ Larson, D. F. , Otsuka, K. , Matsumoto, T. , & Kilic, T. . Should African rural development strategies depend on smallholder farms? An exploration of the inverse – productivity hypothesis. Agricultural Economics, 2014, 45 (3): 355 – 367.

［84］ Masters, W. A. , Djurfeldt, A. A. , De Haan, C. , Hazell, P. , Jayne, T. , Jirström, M. , et al. . Urbanization and farm size in Asia and Africa: Implications for food security and agricultural research. Global Food Security, 2013, 2 (3): 156 – 165.

［85］ HLPE. Investing in smallholder agriculture for food security. A report by The High Level Panel of Experts on Food Security and Nutrition. Rome: FAO, 2013 (6) .

Appendix I : Land Consolidation Questionnaire

Hello! Dear farmers (citizen) Friends:

We are researchers from Sichuan Agricultural University, we are conducting a research on the awareness and perception as well as adaptation intention of smallholder farmers in Sichuan province for optimal production efficiency. In this regard, we are assessing the impact of land consolidation on crop productivity and sustainable development in order to promote possible solutions and recommendations to government and respective organizations. Therefore, your answer for our questionnaire is very important for our findings. Our survey taken anonymously, without leaving a name and address of you do not have any concerns.

Thank you for your support and cooperation!

Research Group of agricultural land management, Sichuan Agricultural University!

Date: _____

Country: _____   Region/Provence: _____

County/Village: _____   Name of data collector: _____

Date of data collection: _____   Household Code: _____

I. Questionnaire at household（HH）level

1. Respondent Name：_____, Sex：M □ F □, Age：_____, Education：_____, how many years live in this village _____, Farming experience：_____ years

2. Main occupation

A）Agriculture □ B）others，specify _____

3. Household Characteristics of the respondent

Household member			Household member Aged			Household member Actively participate in			Annual Income of the HH from（Yuan）		
Total	Male	Female	<18	19－65	>66	On－farm	Off－farm	Non	On－farm	Off－farm	Total

Land Use Pattern（mu）					
Rain fed	Irrigation land	Grassland	Plantation and forest	Perennial crops	Total

4. How are your farmland holding size compare to previous years?

A）Increased □

B）Decreased □

C）No change □

5. If your answer is "A" or "B". What are the reasons?

A）Inheritance/inherited □

B）Allocation/redistribution □

C）Purchased/Sale □

D）Grabbed/expropriated □

E) due to land consolidations ☐

6. Did your landholding certified/licensed?

A) Yes all plots ☐

B) Yes partial ☐

C) Not yet ☐

7. Did you feel land tenure security?

A) Yes ☐

B) No ☐

C) Moderately ☐

8. Did you practice land abandonment (fallow)?

A) Yes ☐why?

B) No ☐

9. Have you rent/shared out your farmland in previous years?

A) Yes ☐why?

B) No ☐

10. Does daily labor a serious problem for you?

A) Yes ☐

B) No ☐

11. Have you experienced with crop failure/damage in your farm plots last years?

A) Yes ☐why?

B) No ☐

12. Have you heard about land consolidation before?

A) Yes ☐

B) No ☐

13. Would you like to merge/consolidate your fragmented farmland holding to a bet-

ter and large one?

A）Yes ☐

B）No☐why?

14. Do you think that land consolidation improve productivity of the land?

A）Yes ☐

B）No ☐

C）I don't know ☐

15. How many plots of land do you cultivated last year?

A）Own _____ plots

B）Rent/shared in _____ plots

C）Rent/shared out _____ plots

II. Farmland characteristics and productivity

Plot Name (the location where the plot found)	Way of Owner-ship (Code A)	Tenure year (years)	Plot Size (mu)	Plot shape (Code B)	Plot steep-press (Code C)	Dista-nce from home-stead	Dist-ance to main road (if yes)	Fert-ility status (Code D)	Soil depth (Code E)	Access to irriga-tion (Code F)	Crop Name (Eg, Rice, wheat., maize)	Crop variety (Code G)	Seed rate used (kg)	Seed price per (kg)	Urea (Nitr-ogen) (kg)	Di-Amm-onium Phos-phate (DAP) (kg)	Man-ure (kg)	Com-post (kg)	Pesti-cide used (L) or (kg)	Own	Hired	Fuel	Own	Hired	Own	Hired	Fuel	Own	Hired	Fuel	Own	Hired	Fuel	Grain Yield (kg)	Straw (stub-ble) Yield (kg)

Column group headers:
- Crop production input used
- Fertilizer rate (kg)
- How many labor and fuel used for land preparation and sowing
- How many labor used for weeding
- How many labor and fuel used for harvesting
- How many labor and fuel used for trashing
- How many labor and fuel used for transporting

Code A
1 = inheritance (own)
2 = allocation by government
3 = rent/shared in
4 = rent/Shared out
5 = purchased
6 = gift from other

Code B
1 = regular shape
2 = irregular shape

Code C
1 = flat
2 = steeply (not flat)

Code D
1 = Fertile
2 = Moderately fertile
3 = Not – fertile

Code E
1 = shallow <20cm
2 = moderate 20 – 60cm
3 = deep >60cm

Code F
1 = yes
2 = no

Crop type Code G:
1 = improved variety
2 = local variety

Remarks:
• Urea Price: _____/100kg
• DAP Price: _____/100kg
• Cost of pesticide: _____/Litter or /kg
• Labor cost: _____ per day/person

III. Structural Equation Model（SEM）Land consolidation Assessment

code	Description of observed variables	Likert scale				
		SDA	DA	UC	A	SA
X1	I have accessed information on land consolidation and rehabilitation from Television and Radio.					
X2	I have accessed information on land consolidation and rehabilitation from Newspapers.					
X3	I have read about land consolidation and rehabilitation from short communication materials（flyers，brochures and posters）.					
X4	I have explored information on land consolidation and rehabilitation from the Internet.					
X5	I discusses about land consolidation and rehabilitation program with my family.					
X6	I discusses with my neighbors or farmers groups about land consolidation and rehabilitation program.					
X7	I discusses with extension workers about land consolidation and rehabilitation program.					
X8	I discuss with my community about land consolidation and rehabilitation program.					
Y1	Land consolidation is the practice of farm plot configuration in terms of size，shape and layout.					
Y2	Land consolidation improves the quality of land for production system including expanding irrigation and drainage systems，road networks which provide better access to plots for both labor and machinery.					
Y3	Land consolidation plays an important role in reducing land degradation as well as improving farmland productivity.					
Y4	Land consolidation reduce social conflict on irrigation water use and farm plot border by improving the irrigation water system and amount, and by providing clear farm plot demarcations among neighbor plots.					
Y5	I am happy and aware of land consolidation and rehabilitation program in my village.					
Y6	Since the establishment of land consolidation and rehabilitation program in my village, the uneconomically dispersed small and irregular farmlands are changed to medium to high quality farmlands.					

Continued Table

code	Description of observed variables	Likert scale				
		SDA	DA	UC	A	SA
Y7	Since the implementation of land consolidation and rehabilitation program in my village, the farm infrastructures such as irrigation and drainage systems, road networks are improving.					
Y8	Since the implementation of land consolidation program in my village, our village becomes clean and tidy and more suitable for residence compares to before.					
Y9	I believe the small, scattered and uneconomical fragmented farmlands will not be appear in my village in future.					
Y10	The land consolidation and rehabilitation program in my village is the responsibility of me, my entire family, village, governmental and non – governmental officials, as well as researchers and academicians.					
Y11	I am always intend to use the recommended fertilizer on my land.					
Y12	I am always intend to use improved crop varieties.					
Y13	I am always intend to rent in neighbor farmland from others.					
Y14	I am always intend to have improve moderate and high quality farmlands.					
Y15	I am always intend to use modern agricultural machinery.					
Y16	I am always intend to have modern irrigation and drainage system in my farmland.					
Y17	I am always intended to have a clean and clear village which is suitable for residence.					

Thank you for your Cooperation!

Appendix II: Land Fragmentation Questionnaire

Dear farmers (citizen) Friends:

Hello! We are researchers from Debre Birhan Agricultural Research Center (DBARC), we are conducting a research on the perspectives and adaptive intention of smallholder farmers to land fragmentation for optimal production efficiency in Ethiopia. In this regard, we are assessing the impact of land fragmentation on crop productivity and income in order to promote possible solutions and recommendations to government and respective organizations. Therefore, your answer for our questionnaire is very important for our findings. Our survey taken anonymously, without leaving a name and address, you do not have any concerns.

Thank you for your support and cooperation!

Research Group of Debre Birhan Agricultural Research center.

Date: _____

Country: _____ Region/Provence: _____

County/Village: _____ Name of data collector: _____

Date of data collection: _____ Household Code: _____

I. Questionnaire at household level

1. Respondent Name: _____ , Sex: M☐ F☐ , Age: _____ , Education: _____ , how many years live in this village _____ , Farming experience: _____ years

2. Main occupation of the household

A) Agriculture ☐ B) others, specify _____

3. Household Characteristics of the respondent

Household member			Household member Aged			Household member Actively participate in			Annual Income of the HH from (Yuan)		
Total	Male	Female	<18	19 – 65	>66	On – farm	Off – farm	non	On – farm	Off – farm	Total

Land Use Pattern (mu)					
Rain fed	Irrigation land	Grassland	Plantation and forest	Perennial crops	Total

4. How are your farmland holding size compare to previous years?

A) Increased ☐

B) Decreased ☐

C) No change ☐

5. If your answer is "A" or "B". What are the reasons?

A) Inheritance/inherited ☐

B) Allocation/redistribution ☐

C) Purchased/Sale ☐

D) Grabbed/expropriated ☐

E) due to land consolidations ☐

6. How many plots of land do you have before land consolidation? _____

7. Did your landholding certified?

A) Yes all plots □

B) Yes partial □

C) Not yet □

8. Did you feel land tenure security?

A) Yes □

B) No □

C) Moderately □

9. Does labor a serious problem for you?

A) Yes □

B) No □

10. Have you experienced with crop failure in your farm plots last years?

A) Yes □why?

B) No □

11. Are you participated land consolidation program implementation?

A) Yes, fully participated □

B) Yes, partially participated □

C) No □

12. Are you satisfied by land consolidation program?

A) Yes □

B) Some □

C) No □

13. If not yes, what are the reasons? _____

———————————————————— .

14. What are the possible solutions you recommend? _____

_____

———————————————————— .

15. How many plots of land do you cultivated last year?

A) Own _____ plots

B) Rent/shared in _____ plots

C) Rent/shared out _____ plots

II. Farmland characteristics and productivity

Plot Name (the location where the plot found)	Way of Owne-rship (Code A)	Tenure year (years)	Plot Size (mu)	Plot shape (Code B)	Plot stee-pness (Code C)	Dista-nce from home-stead	Dist-ance to main road (if yes)	Fert-ility status (Code D)	Soil depth (Code E)	Access to irriga-tion (Code F)	Crop Name (Eg, Rice, wheat, maize)	Crop variety (Code G)	Seed rate used (kg)	Seed price per (kg)	Urea (Nitr-ogen) (kg)	Di-Amm-onium Phos-phate (DAP) (kg)	Man-ure (kg)	Com-post (kg)	Pesti-cide used (L) or (kg)	Own	Hired	Fuel	Own	Hired	Own	Hired	Fuel	Own	Hired	Fuel	Own	Hired	Fuel	Grain Yield (kg)	Straw (stub-ble) Yield (kg)

Column groups: **Fertilizer rate (kg)** spans Urea · Di-Ammonium Phosphate (DAP) · Manure · Compost. Labor/fuel groups: *land preparation and sowing* (Own, Hired, Fuel); *weeding* (Own, Hired); *harvesting* (Own, Hired, Fuel); *trashing* (Own, Hired, Fuel); *transporting* (Own, Hired, Fuel).

Code A:
1 = inheritance (own)
2 = allocation by government
3 = rent/shared in
4 = rent/Shared out
5 = purchased
6 = gift from other

Code B:
1 = regular shape
2 = irregular shape

Code C:
1 = flat
2 = steeply (not flat)

Code D:
1 = Fertile
2 = Moderately fertile
3 = Not – fertile

Code E:
1 = shallow <20cm
2 = moderate 20 – 60cm
3 = deep >60cm

Code F:
1 = yes
2 = no

Crop type Code G:
1 = improved variety
2 = local variety

Remark:
• Urea Price: _____ /100kg
• DAP Price: _____ /100kg
• Cost of pesticide: _____ /Litter or /kg
• Labor cost: _____ per day/person

III. Structural Equation Model (SEM) Land Consolidation Assessment

code	Description of observed variables	Likert scale				
		SDA	DA	UC	A	SA
X1	Perceived risk of land fragmentation on land degradation and soil erosion					
X2	Perceived risk of land fragmentation on to investments in land (inputs use, management) and follow – up activities					
X3	Perceived risk of land fragmentation on modern agricultural infrastructure and mechanization system					
X4	Perceived risk of land fragmentation on cost of production (labor, time)					
X5	Perceived risk of land fragmentation on conflict on the boundary with neighbor land owners					
X6	Perceived pressure from family and relatives					
X7	Perceived pressure from neighbor and farmers group (cell) (i. e. one cell has five members)					
X8	Perceived pressure from agricultural extension agents					
X9	Perceived pressure from the community members of the village					
X10	Land shared/rent in/out is an adaptive option to reduce land fragmentation risks					
X11	Land fallowing practice is an adaptive option to reduce the risks of land fragmentation					
X12	Land use change (crop land to plantation land) is an alternative adaptive option to reduce the risks of land fragmentation					
X13	Utilization of farm inputs and management practices are an alternative adaptive option to reduce the risks of land fragmentation					
X14	The land management activities (terracing, planting) in my village encourage for adaptive intentions					
X15	Access to the market and bank/credit centers in my village inspire for adaptive intentions					
X16	Access to the agricultural/health/school services in my village motivate for adaptive intentions					

Continued Table

code	Description of observed variables	Likert scale				
		SDA	DA	UC	A	SA
Y1	I always intend to merge and consolidate the scattered farm parcels to larger and better shaped parcel					
Y2	I always intend to have moderate to high quality farm parcel and free of land and soil degradation threats					
Y3	I always intend to have access to irrigation and drainage system and road network in my parcels					
Y4	I always intend to use modern agricultural mechanization					
Y5	I always intend to use the recommended farm inputs (fertilizer, variety, seed rate) for better production					
K1	Farm size holding of the household					
K2	The number of farm plot holding of the households					
K3	The land fragmentation status of the farm household					
K4	The crop diversification system of the household					

Thank you for your Cooperation!

Abbreviation Index

FAO Food and Agricultural Organization

SEM Structural Equation Modeling

LULC Land Use Land Cover

GDP Gross Domestic Product

FDRE Federal Democratic Republic of Ethiopia

LCRC Land Consolidation and Rehabilitation Center

EEA Ethiopian Economic Association

ERSS Ethiopian Rural Security Survey

HRS Household Responsibility System

CPC Communist Party of China

EPRDF Ethiopian People Revolutionary Democratic Front

MLRA Ministry of Land Reform and Administration

NBS National Bureau of Statistics of China

FYSP Five Year Strategic Plan

TPB Theory of Planned Behavior

TRA Theory of Reasoned Action

TAM   Technology Acceptance Model

GIS   Geographic Information System

FHM   Farm Household Models

SPFM   Stochastic Production Frontier Model

GLM   General Linear Model

SBS   Statistics Bureau of Sichuan